SCOTLAND AND THE UNION

THE DAVID HUME INSTITUTE

Hume Papers on Public Policy
Volume 2 No 2 Summer 1994

SCOTLAND AND THE UNION

Edited by
Patrick S Hodge

EDINBURGH UNIVERSITY PRESS

Edinburgh University Press
22 George Square, Edinburgh
Transferred to digital print 2008
Typeset in Times New Roman by ROM-Data Corporation Ltd.,
Falmouth, Cornwall and printed and bound in Great Britain
by CPI Antony Rowe, Eastbourne, East Sussex

A CIP record for this book is available from the
British Library

ISBN 0 7486 0510 X

Contents

Contributors

Sir Gerald Elliot is Chairman of the Board of Trustees of The David Hume Institute. He is an industrialist and was formerly Chairman of Christian Salvesen plc.

Professor Andrew Bain is Professor of Economics in the University of Glasgow.

Dr David King is Senior Lecturer in the Department of Economics in the University of Stirling.

Sir John Thomson is Chairman of Minorities Rights Group International. He is a retired diplomat and was formerly British Permanent Representative to the United Nations.

Professor Roy Campbell is Emeritus Professor of Economic History in the University of Stirling.

Dr John Morrill is a Fellow and Vice Master of Selwyn College, Cambridge. He is a Reader in Early Modern History in the University of Cambridge.

Professor Colin Munro is Professor of Constitutional Law in the University of Edinburgh.

Allan Massie is an author and journalist. He is Honorary Vice President of The David Hume Institute.

Patrick Hodge is a member of the Faculty of Advocates.

Foreword

It sometimes seems that the case for the continuation of the Union of 1707 is simply ignored or belittled by those who oppose it. Thus Paul Scott (1992a: 55) has written of those who defend the Union that 'they produce no satisfactory explanation of this position, which is more an act of faith than a reasonable policy'. Again Andrew Marr (1992: 240) states: 'Because I cannot take the central political arguments against Scottish Home Rule seriously, I remain of the view that it will one day come about.' Although the heady days preceding the General Election of 1992, when some thought independence imminent, may now seem somewhat remote, both history and events since the election suggest that the issue of Scottish self-government is unlikely to disappear. In the present work Patrick Hodge has gathered together a team of distinguished writers who provide thoughtful, serious and carefully-researched arguments in defence of the Union, although not necessarily of the status quo. In consequence it should henceforth be impossible to make remarks such as those of Scott and Marr quoted above if the case for Scottish independence is to retain true intellectual integrity. Naturally, and as always, The David Hume Institute takes no collective view on the merits of the arguments here put forward, or of those which may be opposed to them. The Institute has however always prided itself on the fact that it is a Scottish and not a metropolitan organisation, and it is a pleasure to assist in this important contribution to the debate about how Scotland should be governed.

Hector L MacQueen
Executive Director
The David Hume Institute

Editor's Foreword

The purpose of this small book of essays is to make a contribution to the debate on the future government of Scotland from a unionist perspective.

The eight contributors whom I recruited are people who have an interest in Scottish affairs but who are not actively involved in party politics and are therefore not constrained by an adopted policy. Each has written an essay on Scotland in their own area of interest, whether business, economics, international relations, law or history.

I wish to record my gratitude to the late Professor Gordon Donaldson, the Historiographer Royal, who had agreed to write an essay on the Union from an historical perspective but who sadly died before his essay was written. Professor Roy Campbell and Dr John Morrill undertook at short notice to produce historical contributions in his place.

I am grateful also to Mrs Janet Buchanan Smith and Mrs Clare Graaf who encouraged me to embark on this project in March 1992 when I discussed the possibility with them. My thanks are also due to Dr Hector MacQueen at The David Hume Institute for arranging publication, to Kathy Mountain for preparing the texts for the press, to Eugenio da Costa e Silva for research assistance, and to my secretary Mrs Moira Paton who typed my extensive correspondence and my small contribution to the book.

Patrick S Hodge

Introduction

Patrick S Hodge

The idea of this book arose in the Spring of 1992 before the General Election. At that time there was much media coverage of the nationalist arguments but few voices were raised arguing the case for the continuance of the Union. While politics have moved on, the continuing economic integration and likely political development of the European Union (EU) make the structure of the United Kingdom (UK) government and the future role of the Westminster Parliament important issues for discussion. The elections of 1994 – European Parliament, local government and the Monklands by-election – have all suggested that the form of Scottish government remains a live political question.

The book comprises eight essays. It begins with three essays on economic questions which deal respectively with industry, financial institutions and the general economy. The fourth essay discusses the representation of Scottish interests in international affairs. Then one Scottish and one English historian consider from their different perspectives the background and consequences of the Union of 1707. The seventh contribution, by a constitutional lawyer, provides a legal analysis of the British constitution. The final essay is an examination of the development of a British culture and its contribution to Scottish identity. Each of the essays argues for the continuing validity of the Union formed in 1707, although that is not to say that all the contributors subscribe to the status quo.

In sum, the first four essays suggest that independence would impose significant financial and other costs on Scotland, which would outweigh possible benefits. The last four essays call into question some of the beliefs and assumptions which underlie Scottish nationalism, and in particular, nationalist views of Scottish cultural identity.

Economic Arguments

The benefit of the Union to the Scottish economy was among the strongest arguments in its favour when the Union was negotiated. 'Trade with most ....' was the Earl of Roxburgh's contemporary judgment of the motives of the majority of the Scottish Parliamentarians in favour of the Union of 1707. In the twentieth century political pressure for constitutional change in Scotland has periodically ebbed and flowed, increasing in the latter part of the century.

But the Scottish business community has shown no enthusiasm for devolutionary initiatives, and open hostility to Scottish independence.

The first three essays in this compilation set out economic arguments which question the material benefits to be derived from independence. These identify significant costs which may be a consequence of separation from the UK.

Scottish Industry

The benefit of free access to larger and more prosperous markets was a powerful argument in favour of the Union at the outset. It remains so. In his essay Sir Gerald Elliot, an industrialist, articulates views which are held by many in Scottish industry. First, he emphasises the need to maintain an integrated UK economy. Scottish industry is dependent on international trade because the majority of its markets is outwith Scotland. The economic integration of the UK provides opportunities for Scottish business. Networks of commercial and personal relationships have developed which transcend the boundaries of Scotland. Secondly, the consumer has benefited significantly from the existence of free trade within the UK and from the development of relatively free trade internationally. These benefits should be preserved. Where a state seeks to protect the interests of its producers, this is usually at the expense of the consumer. Thirdly, the economic interdependence of the constituent parts of the UK and of the UK with other states, particularly within the EU, is now an important constraint on the scope of economic policy of the UK Government. It would be even greater for a Scottish Government. It is likely that if a Scottish Government pursued industrial policies which diverged significantly from the policies of the rest of the UK, it would need to introduce controls to fence off the Scottish economy. The freedom to pursue an independent economic policy would impose significant costs on Scottish industry and on Scottish consumers.

Financial Services

The hostility of the Scottish financial sector to major alteration of the constitutional status quo is well known. The publication before the 1992 General Election of the Pieda study of the Scottish economy (Bell Lawrie White 1992) generated considerable political controversy. In particular the suggestion that Scottish quoted and investment-oriented businesses had considered moving their head offices out of Scotland in response to devolution or independence attracted comment.

The economist, Professor Andrew Bain, examines the nature, scale and significance of the Scottish financial sector, which employs about 77,000 people and is a major service export industry. He analyses the problems which independence and the creation of a separate currency would create. The banks and life assurance companies would be likely to face significant transitional problems before, during and after the creation of a separate currency. The most important market of the Scottish life assurance companies is the rest of the UK. Independence would therefore be likely to cause permanent damage to the Scottish life assurance industry through the loss of new business from England.

To avoid this risk of permanent damage, it would be in the interest of some companies to shift their country of incorporation to England. Some investment fund managers would be likely to face similar, though less severe, problems. The threat of disadvantageous tax rates, whether or not they eventuated, could also cause at least temporary problems for Scottish life assurance companies. Any move towards higher rates of personal taxation in Scotland would have an adverse impact on the operating costs of Scottish fund managers. Even the possibility of this occurring might affect their ability to attract to Scotland qualified employees who could obtain employment elsewhere.

Of these problems, the threat of permanent damage to major Scottish institutions' access to the English market is the most serious. Scotland's financial institutions depend on the continued economic integration of the UK and are likely to remain hostile to any political initiative which threatens that integrity. Accordingly they might be hostile even to devolution, if it were seen as a prelude to independence rather than as part of a UK-wide decentralisation.

It appears therefore that in the present structure of the EU independence is likely to impose heavy costs both on Scottish industry and on Scotland's financial sector. If the EU achieves monetary union, some of the serious economic problems which independence would pose might be avoided. But there would be little scope for any Member State – and particularly a small Member State – to pursue within the monetary union a significantly independent economic policy. This causes an economist to ask the question, 'Where is the benefit of independence?'.

Economics

Dr David King, an economist, examines the scope for a Scottish Government to pursue independent economic policies if Scotland remained within the EU. He argues that an independent Scotland would probably be admitted to the EU only if it agreed to participate in monetary union when that occurs. And when it does occur, he believes that all EU members will find it difficult to pursue independent economic policies. Indeed, this is the main reason that some elements of the Conservative party are so hostile to monetary union.

He begins by examining the performance of the Scottish economy and finds that Scotland is currently one of the more prosperous regions of the UK. He then examines the scope for independent economic policies under three categories, namely stabilisation (the regulation of demand to influence unemployment and inflation), redistribution and resource allocation.

It is notoriously difficult for any national government to pursue successful stabilisation policies. The recession which has afflicted most OECD countries vouches for the difficulty. The problems are greatest for small economies where imports and international capital flows are relatively important, especially if there are no controls over imports or capital flows. In such economies, any attempt to alter demand and domestic output by using fiscal or monetary policy may lead chiefly to a change in the level of imports. Moreover, there may be very little scope for setting independent interest rates and so very little scope for even attempting an independent monetary policy. An independent

Scotland might seek to create some scope for an independent monetary policy by reimposing capital controls, but this is unlikely to be permitted by the EU. In any event that would threaten Scotland's financial sector. Alternatively, it might seek to raise demand by reducing the exchange rate of its currency. But Irish experience suggests that a policy of depreciation leads to increases in domestic prices.

The difficulties would be greatly compounded by monetary union. It is widely accepted that once that occurs, all EU members will be largely unable to pursue their own stabilisation policies. With monetary union, there will be a single European currency regulated by a central EU bank, so members will have no scope for independent monetary policies or exchange rate policies. The EU is already urging governments to limit their borrowing which in turn curtails fiscal policy.

A Scottish Government would be likely to have only limited scope for independent redistribution policies. Scotland will have close links with the rest of the UK and the EU. If a Scottish Government imposed higher taxes on its wealthier citizens to finance more generous transfers to the poor, the former might be tempted to vote with their feet and leave. Moreover, assuming that an independent Scotland signed up to the Maastricht treaty, it would find even more curbs on its independence.

In the field of resource allocation, King sees much more scope for independent policies. An independent Scotland could certainly adopt its own policies over the ownership and finance of the water industry and over public services such as education and health. But King wonders whether much of the control of these activities might not best be entrusted to smaller authorities within Scotland to bring decisions even closer to the people.

King's chief conclusion, then, is that, once monetary union has taken place within the EU, there will be little scope for independent stabilisation policies by any member government. To secure any substantial freedom of action, Scotland would have to secede from the EU as well as the UK. It is not clear how much support there would be for this within Scotland, especially now that most of the west European non-members of the EU seem set to join.

International Relations

Economic arguments are only one part of a range of arguments which are advanced for or against the Union. There may be circumstances in which even significant prejudice to a nation's economy is a price worth paying for a desired benefit from independence. Are there such benefits for Scotland?

One field which requires examination is that of international relations. It has been argued that Scottish interests would be advanced more successfully in international affairs if Scotland were independent. 'A small voice is better than no voice at all' (Scott 1992a: 44).

The former diplomat Sir John Thomson considers these arguments. He sets out three options available to Scotland, as an independent country within the EU; as an independent country outside the EU; and as a constituent nation of the UK.

At present Scotland's voice may be heard on the international stage indirectly, mediated through the voice of the UK. No doubt as part of the UK, Scotland's interests require to be weighed up along with other UK interests. As a result on some occasions Scotland's interests will prevail and on others they must give way. But the UK is one of the larger Member States of, and is a substantial net contributor to the EU. It is also a country which for historical and other reasons has greater clout than the size of its economy would suggest. As a result the UK enjoys a much greater international influence than Scotland could aspire to.

A Scottish Government would require to establish a separate diplomatic service and defence forces for an independent Scotland and would incur significantly increased costs as a result. Independence would involve Scotland in negotiating a divorce from its larger and more powerful neighbour. Few divorces are amicable and Scotland would be in a relatively weak position in such negotiations. Further, it is likely that an independent Scotland would be involved in at least some negotiations in order to become a member of the EU in circumstances where the break-up of Member States within the EU might be seen as damaging to Europe and where Scotland would be only one of several small states seeking membership.

Scottish nationalists – drawing on and updating the ideas of Andrew Fletcher of Saltoun about three hundred years ago – have advanced the argument that Scotland could join with other small states within the EU to curb the power of the larger Member States. Thomson questions this view. On the one hand he doubts whether voters in Scotland favour much closer European integration any more than voters in other Member States. On the other hand he suggests that the smaller Member States, being geographically and economically disparate, will not find it easy to combine as a bloc within the EU. As the number of members grows, so the relative importance of each of the small states will decrease, while the influence of the five major states will remain the same or increase.

He concludes that it would probably not be sensible for Scotland to opt for independence outside the EU. Independence within the EU means giving up at least as much sovereignty and control as is involved already in membership of the UK. In terms of international relations, although Scotland would have a vote in the EU, it could expect the Scottish voice to be less influential than if expressed through the UK. He also notes the likelihood of serious divisions within the Scottish nation in the process of arranging for independence whether within or outwith the EU. On balance he concludes that independence is likely to be costly for Scotland's international relations while simultaneously resulting in less effective representation of its interests.

Historical Arguments

It is necessary to consider other supposed benefits of independence for Scotland. One such benefit is the preservation and advancement of Scottish culture. None of the contributors to this book challenge the view that Scotland is a nation and that there are features of Scottish culture which are distinct from the cultures of the other parts of the UK. It is, however, notoriously difficult to determine what we mean by nationality, culture and identity in Scotland – or anywhere else.

Nationalism has been defined as 'a political movement which seeks to attain and defend an objective which we may call national integrity' (Minogue 1967: 25). National integrity, like national identity, is difficult to define. Nationalists often tend to exaggerate not only the distinctiveness but also the coherence of the national culture they seek to protect. In order to give political content to their perception of national identity, nationalists frequently adopt a tendentious portrayal of the past. In his celebrated, and unsympathetic, study of nationalism Eric Hobsbawm (1990: 12) put the point more forcefully:

> Nationalism required too much belief in what is patently not so ... Getting its history wrong is part of being a nation.

In Scotland, the argument is often advanced that independence is necessary to preserve Scottish culture and Scottish identity from the elephantine weight of English culture. (See for example Scott 1991: 49-76).

History plays a central role in the debate in this field. The next three essays, by the historians Professor Roy Campbell and Dr John Morrill and by the constitutional lawyer Professor Colin Munro, seek to set the Union in its historical context and in so doing call into question some of the historical arguments which have been advanced in favour of independence.

Although there are clear differences in the traditions of Scotland and England, there were close ties between the two countries from at latest the middle ages. The Anglo-Norman aristocracy played an important role in the establishment of the Scottish kingdom. Recent historical research has shown that it is essential to an understanding of politics and society in the medieval British Isles to appreciate the close links of the aristocracies of England and Scotland in the formative years of both kingdoms. These links included ties of marriage, extensive land holdings in both kingdoms and in France, and connections with more than one royal court. Davies (1988) and Frame (1990) have argued persuasively that the strength of the royal and noble heritages across the boundaries within the British Isles created a common culture in the four medieval cores in lowland England, lowland Scotland, the Englishries of Wales and the Pale in Ireland. Each nation's history should be seen in a British context. The common law of Scotland in the middle ages involved a, no doubt discriminating, borrowing and adaptation of Anglo-Norman law from the successful English monarchy (MacQueen 1993; Sellar 1988). Further as Morrill points out, lowland Scotland, the heartland of the medieval and early modern kingdom, in part drew its language, social norms and religious culture from Normandy.

The Union was preceded by a long process of assimilation of Scotland and England. The dynastic ties forged in the sixteenth century led to the Union of the Crowns of 1603. Of central importance was the Reformation. It was not just a desire to escape from French ambitions to colonise Scotland but shared protestantism which caused Scottish politicians to turn to England in the mid-sixteenth century (Donaldson 1985). Protestantism also led directly to the King James Bible. Modern studies of nationalism (Anderson 1991; Hobsbawm 1990) have emphasised the importance of a common language and in particular the written word in the development of a national identity. The Bible written in English played a central role in the creation of a British culture. The Union of the Crowns did not prove a satisfactory settlement of Anglo-Scottish relations. There were disputes over religion until the two protestant kingdoms agreed to differ on the form of Church government in the revolution settlement of 1689. On the economic front the Scottish Government found it impossible to pursue successfully an independent economic policy against the interests of the Westminster Parliament and the City of London. The Union of 1707 was agreed upon as a remedy for long-standing problems in the relations between Scotland and England as well as the short-term need to secure an agreed succession to the throne. While the English negotiators may have insisted on an incorporating union, it was not the English but the Scots, including even the covenanting leadership, who had attempted repeatedly in the seventeenth century to put Scotland's relationship with its larger neighbour on a more established and secure basis. Further Scotland obtained the much-needed access to the English and colonial markets which contributed greatly to its industrial success within the Union.

The Union was not an attempt to achieve a complete assimilation of Scotland with England. Munro discusses the continuance of Scottish national identity in the Church, the law and civil society. Each changed over time. The Kirk played a central role in Scottish identity until the Disruption of 1843, which was 'the death of the godly vision', and increasing secularization weakened its role (Storrar 1990). Scots law has retained much of its independence. Harmonisation with English law has occurred principally in the field of commercial law and frequently in response to initiatives not from London but from influential Scots lawyers and businessmen (Rodger 1992). Harmonisation of commercial law is now pursued by and within the EU. Further, while the Union gave rise to some further cultural assimilation, a sense of Scottish identity remains strong. In reality Queen Anne's 'entire and perfect Union' was neither sought nor achieved. The qualified nature of the Union has preserved in being institutions which tend to approach problems principally or solely from a Scottish standpoint.

Campbell attributes the increasing stress on Scottish distinctiveness and the relative economic decline of the UK in the twentieth century as causes of increasing political introversion in Scotland. This isolationism, he warns, threatens the Union and may lead to a result which most people in Scotland do not want.

National sentiment often rests on a belief that a people within a defined geographical area form a community (Seton Watson 1977: 5). However, a nation is at best an extremely abstract kind of community; even a small nation is too large and contains too diverse a population to be anything other than 'an imagined political community' (Anderson 1991: 6).

Some of the stories which have underpinned national sentiment to create this imagined political community are simply myths. Such myths may either be historically untrue (such as the Swiss story of William Tell) or else an idealisation of fact. Other stories are mere assertions which have an unreliable historical basis or are not a balanced assessment of historical fact. One example of the latter is the presentation of the Union as the triumph of a long-pursued English scheme to dominate Scotland. Morrill's paper provides a refutation of this view.

Another is the assertion that the Union was achieved principally through bribery and intimidation. This assertion has a long pedigree:

> We're bought and sold for English gold –
> Such a parcel of rogues in a nation!

It survives in one of Paul H Scott's modern nationalist booklets (Scott 1992a: 23), although it is qualified in his historical study of Andrew Fletcher and the Union (Scott 1992b). The Scottish politicians who supported the Union and risked the anger of the mob were not selling their birthright for a mess of pottage (Speck 1994: ch 6). The reality behind the Union was a combination of, on the one hand, the pursuit of Scottish economic interests and the benefits of political stability, and, on the other, political manipulation and Government patronage. The latter was part and parcel of politics at that time, and at other times.

Those who favour independence often assert that, as a multi-nation state, the UK is an anomaly (Scott 1992a: 27). This is unfounded in fact. On the contrary, many modern states contain several nations and several cultures. France and Spain are clear examples, with Brittany and Catalonia among others being nations within a larger state. Italy is a state which was created by a political movement before an Italian national identity had been developed among its people. 'We have made Italy, now we have to make Italians' were the words of Massimo d'Azeglio (Seton Watson 1977: 107). Germany has components such as Saxony and Bavaria with a long history of distinctive identity. Accordingly it is truer to say that the UK as a multi-nation state is an example of the European norm.

That Scottish culture is distinctive and valuable is not in dispute. However, the degree of distinctiveness may often be overstated. George Davie's (1961) influential thesis on Scottish university education highlighted the role of a broad philosophical education in the Scottish universities at the time of the Scottish Enlightenment and in the early nineteenth century. He lamented the anglicisation of the Scottish universities from the mid-nineteenth century onwards and the development of a more specialised and less philosophical education. His works have contributed to the belief that Scotland formerly possessed an education system which was open to children of all classes and permitted social mobility between the classes. However, more recent historical research into education and opportunity in Victorian Scotland strongly suggests that any supposed golden age of opportunity by educational advancement never existed (Anderson 1989). By the mid-nineteenth century Scotland's economic development required, not a broadly-based philosophical education, but one which gave due weight to modern science and mathematics (Campbell 1980: 41-52). Whatever the reality, the idea of such a philosophical education was by then out-dated. Further the belief that there was significantly greater social mobility in Scotland than in England, the myth of the 'lad o' pairts', has on closer examination been found to be overstated. While social advancement through education may have been available to a wider range of the middle classes in Scotland than in England, opportunities for advancement from the working classes remained few in both countries.

The structure of Scottish society is strikingly similiar to that of other parts of Britain. This may not be surprising as Scotland is, like other parts of the UK, an advanced industrial society. Scotland had in the later nineteenth century, and has retained, a similar profile of industrial employment to Britain as a whole, a similar occupational structure and a similar proportion of women in employment. Its patterns of social class and social mobility are shared with other parts of Britain (McCrone 1992: chs 3 and 4). Accordingly neither social nor economic structure provides clear support for Scotland's egalitarian myth, which may be more a social ethos than an analysis of fact. It is certainly not a convincing explanation for the divergence of voting behaviour between Scotland and the rest of the UK in recent years.

Constitutional Law

As Munro points out in his essay on Scotland's constitutional position, the Union which created the British state was not an attempt to create a homogeneous British nation. The similarities between Scotland and the rest of the UK are not the result of any grand policy of assimilation but are largely the product of long-established ties, piecemeal initiatives and circumstance.

If the creators of the Union legislation intended to make at least some of its provisions unalterable laws, they did not succeed. Subsequent parliamentary legislation *has* significantly altered, and often for the better, the provisions of the Treaty of Union. Further while the Scottish Courts have been equivocal in their pronouncements on the status of the Treaty they have never held a later statutory provision invalid on the ground that it breached one of its articles. This may be contrasted with the attitude of the British Courts to UK legislation within the sphere of competence of the EU, where UK legislation has been declared inapplicable when it contravened European Community law.

The relationship of Scotland with the rest of the UK has therefore not been secured by any 'Basic Law' or other special constitutional provision. Nevertheless, Munro argues that the nationhood of Scotland within the UK has received constitutional recognition in a number of ways. First, the preservation of Scots law as a separate legal system has upheld a distinctive symbol of national identity. Secondly, within Parliament there has been a practice of introducing separate legislation for Scotland in relation to certain matters, and there are separate legislative procedures for such Scottish measures. However, shortage of Parliamentary time has hampered the enactment of Scottish provisions. This has given rise to criticism, which is not without foundation, of failure to reform Scots law by implementing the proposals of the Scottish

Law Commission. Thirdly, the high degree of administrative devolution introduced since the late nineteenth century has contributed to Scotland enjoying a higher expenditure *per capita* than other parts of Great Britain. Further there has remained in Scotland a distinctive civil society involving the Kirk, the legal profession, the separate education system, a Scotland-oriented media and distinctive architectural traditions.

Government in Britain has continued to undergo reform. The intensification of government activity has been followed by the extension of judicial supervision of its decision-making. The courts have since the 1940s developed new judicial review doctrines. The 1970s and 1980s saw the introduction of quicker court procedures for judicial review in both Scotland and England. This has encouraged the Civil Service to be aware of the scope for judicial challenge to its actings and in a pamphlet entitled *The judge over your shoulder* (Cabinet Office 1987) to instruct its officials on the constraints imposed on them by the law. If government cannot be made to be good, it can at least be made to follow proper procedure; and accountability is thereby increased.

The contributors to this book do not dispute that further reform is needed. Rolling back the frontiers of the state in the 1980s had some paradoxical results. For example, changes to the structure and finance of local government led, in some respects at least, to centralisation of power and decision-making in Whitehall and associated quangos. There remains scope for further reform of government without breaking up Britain or destroying the integrity of the UK economy. Several contributors argue for greater decentralisation throughout the UK. Many of the benefits, for which advocates of independence argue, may be achieved by less radical measures. UK-wide decentralisation, a strengthening of local government and reform of parliamentary procedures to ensure adequate time for Scottish measures could achieve much.

Scottish Culture and British Culture

The fact that a considerable majority of Scottish voters in General Elections has continued to vote for the UK parties and has not favoured the option of independence may indicate not only a belief that the British State can meet its demands but also an awareness of the cultural ties which in recent years have been overshadowed by an emphasis on our cultural distinctiveness. In the final essay, the author and journalist Allan Massie examines the cultural community which has grown up between Scotland and England over many centuries. This community is not simply a product of the Union. The Union has built on what Scotland and England already had in common.

Contrary to what is often asserted by Scottish nationalists, Scotland was not and is not 'more European' than England. In the middle ages Scotland and England shared in the common feudal culture of Western Europe. Both countries have long had strong cultural links with the Continent. Of the several strands in Scottish culture the Celtic strain in the highlands is the most distinct from that of England. Yet this separates highland Scotland as much from

Europe as from England. It has also separated the highlands from the lowlands in Scotland since at least the fourteenth century. The Scots language, which became the official language of administration in late medieval Scotland, was a brand of English having developed out of North English. There was little difference between the language spoken on either side of the Border in this period.

Cultural ties were greatly strengthened when the Scottish kingdom shifted its political alliance from France to England at the Reformation. The close links with England, which were created by the Reformation, had a profound effect on Scottish culture for three hundred years. These developments formed the cultural backdrop to and help explain the attempts in the seventeenth century, especially by leading Scottish politicians, to create a political structure in Britain which would secure the co-operation of England and Scotland in the longer term.

Following the Union of 1707 the main Scottish institutions were left in Scottish hands. At the same time a process of assimilation occurred whereby leading literary figures from different parts of Britain exercised a profound influence on each other. Massie points to major figures such as Dr John Arbuthnott and James Thomson as evidence of a community of culture in eighteenth-century Britain. Even the ersatz Gaelic culture of Macpherson's 'Ossian' appealed to a taste for Celtic mythology which was already well established throughout Britain. On a higher plane there were close ties between eighteenth-century philosophers and historians such as Smith, Hume and Gibbon.

The French Revolution and the resulting disruption on the Continent strengthened the idea of Britain and British culture. Burke and Macaulay, respectively Irish and Scottish by descent, were both British writers. In the nineteenth century and afterwards the cross-fertilisation of cultures continued with Scots writers such as Scott, Carlyle and Stevenson having easily as much influence on English culture as English writers had on Scotland. The role of the Scots in the BBC in the twentieth century, and in particular Lord Reith, is well known. Migration in both directions across the border has strengthened the cultural community.

This cultural community has developed and exists independent of the political organisation of the British State. Professor Linda Colley (1992: 374-75) has argued persuasively that the forces which shaped British political identity in the eighteenth century, namely protestantism, the external threat posed by France and the commercial opportunities of Empire, have either declined in influence or ceased to operate and that a substantial re-thinking of what it is to be British is needed. She sees Great Britain as an invented nation superimposed on much older alignments and loyalties. However, it is important to realise two points in considering this argument. The older alignments and loyalties of which she speaks included, as Massie argues, a substantial community of culture within Britain, regardless of political structure. Also the component parts of Britain, including Scotland, have themselves changed irrevocably since the Union. The Kirk, which played a central role in Scottish life between the sixteenth and nineteenth centuries, has suffered a calamitous loss of influence. In all parts of Britain, secularisation has altered fundamentally the nature of our society, and probably nowhere more than in Scotland, which has been described as 'part of the modern, agnostic, consumer, capitalist society, facing problems of resource shortage, and potential nuclear extinction' (Smout 1977: 11). The uncertain search for a role and for a new identity is thus not confined to apologists for the British State but affects those who, with intellectual honesty, argue for a return to Welshness or Scottishness.

Conclusion

Economic arguments which loomed large at the time of the Union remain an important part of the Scottish debate. Scottish nationalists have not as yet, put forward a convincing economic case for separation. In particular, reliance on the single European market does not give enough weight to the many barriers to trade within that market. Nor does it deal with the problem that, after independence, many Scottish products, in particular financial products, would be perceived as foreign in their most important markets, *viz* the rest of Britain.

It is likely that the integration of the European economy and the harmonisation of the commercial laws of Member States of the EU will continue, even if only faltering progress is made towards political integration. In that context it is difficult to see how the costs – both financial and otherwise – involved in separation from the UK to create a small nation state within the EU can be justified on economic grounds.

Further, it is far from self-evident that the pursuit of independence is the road to a better society in Scotland. Tolerance and pluralism are widely perceived as virtues in the Western world. In this book it is argued that as a general rule a multi-nation state is more likely to secure tolerance and pluralistic democracy than a nation state where government is legitimated by nationalism. That is not to say – as some have done – that nationalism is necessarily evil. In a recent David Hume Institute paper Professor Neil MacCormick (1994) has argued for a liberal nationalism which respects pluralism and protects minorities. Nationalism, he argues, may be compatible with individualism as individuals have their identity in the context of a particular society and culture in which they live. However he recognises, as the history of the later twentieth century so amply demonstrates, that it is profoundly difficult to secure acceptance only of liberal nationalist principles (MacCormick 1994: 95).

It is not a sufficient answer – as others would have it – to the critics of nationalism to say that it is not nationalism but only imperialism – where one nation seeks to assert its power over another – which is a moral evil. That argument ignores – as MacCormick does not – the internally divisive tendency in many nationalist movements, through their emphasis on what is allegedly distinct in their culture, to deny the heterogeneous nature of their society and that part of their identity which is shared with their neighbours. Such movements tend to exclude or disregard the interests of those of their citizens who perceive themselves in terms of the shared identity or who have a cultural identity different from the politically favoured norm. The example of the Slovak Republic and its Magyar minority is one of many.

In Scotland, nationalism has been blighted by anti-English sentiment despite the worthy efforts of its political leadership. The contributors to this book challenge several of the beliefs which are prevalent in Scottish nationalist writing. One which is not examined but which is worthy of study is the simplistic contrast drawn between characteristics which are said to be Scottish and those which are attributed to the English. Not only is Scottishness an ill-defined concept but also there is a failure when speaking of 'the English' to appreciate the heterogeneous nature of English society. The stereotype of many Scottish criticisms is a member of the south-eastern metropolitan elite. There is a failure to appreciate the geographical diversity of English culture and society and a failure to recognise how much lowland Scottish society and culture have in common in particular with the north of England. While it may be gratifying to compare ourselves with a demonised stereotype, it does little to reveal the truth.

If voters in Scotland seek to alter fundamentally the structure of their government, it is important that they do so with their eyes open not only to the benefits but also to the costs – and not just the economic costs. And it is essential that those who campaign for or against such radical change should present the options in an open way. In a recent profile of Nelson Mandela in *The Independent on Sunday* (1 May 1994) Neal Ascherson stated:

> Mandela does have some of the qualities of Thomas Masaryk, who brought the Czechs and Slovaks to independence in 1918. There is the same fanatical attachment to truth, as if freedom achieved by lies, bombast and deceit were not worth having.

If we have that attachment to truth, may we not recognise that there are many Scots – perhaps the majority – who feel strongly about Scotland as a nation, but who consider that it can best express itself within the UK? May it not be that those who pursue independence overlook the divisiveness of that policy within Scotland, and underestimate the bitterness which a break from the rest of Britain would create?

What we have in common with people from other parts of Britain far outweighs our differences. The continuing process of European integration is creating opportunities for the Member States of the EU to re-organise the distribution of political power within their borders. It is not clear whether and to what extent this will lead to constitutional change in Britain. However a political structure which recognises our plural identity – Scottish, British and European – is one which is likely to foster liberalism and pluralist democracy. A nationalism which rests on a partial view of our history and identity, far from emancipating, may diminish us.

Separation – For Richer or For Poorer?

Gerald Elliot

When the last intensive round of debate on constitutional reform in Scotland took place, on the occasion of the 1992 general election, it seemed to surprise nationalists, devolutionists and their supporters in the press that business people in Scotland showed virtually no interest in constitutional change. No industrial leaders of weight came out on the Scottish Nationalist side, and those few that declared for devolution seemed to be simply following the sound business practice of adjusting in good time to what seemed to be inevitable. So the promoters of devolution through the Constitutional Convention were left to draft their manifesto without the advice or support of the commercial community.

This essay will discuss why changes in the organisation of government, even if adorned with a bright patriotic badge, strike so faint a spark among those who work in commerce and industry. It will also pursue the question of what size and shape of government can best serve society's aims to bring increasing prosperity to its members at a high level of employment. Is the present pressure towards smaller and more independent units of government for 'running our own affairs', whether Asturias, Scotland or Shetland, compatible with the stronger urge for improved material well-being?

The arguments about devolution or separation have many aspects. The effects on creation of wealth are only part of the picture. But it is an important part. In making decisions on how they should be governed most people give priority to their material welfare. So they will judge any new system of government by the contribution it can make to this.

Scottish industry has transformed in the past half century. We started out after the war with steel, heavy engineering, mining and textiles predominant. For some of these industries the war temporarily arrested a decline that had already set in. In the 1950s and 1960s coal, ship building and steel passed into state ownership. At the time this was proclaimed as the takeover for public benefit of the 'commanding heights of the economy'. In historical perspective it looks more like a desperate attempt to protect these industries from a shrinking that was inevitable. Nationalisation probably hastened their decline, making them unable to adapt to changing conditions until it was too late. Meanwhile new industries were growing up, some of them created by inward investment from outside the UK, first from the USA, more recently from Japan. Electronics, food processing, light engineering, financial services developed. In the early 1970s the discovery and development of offshore oil brought to Scotland a new industry of massive scale, not only introducing its own technologies but providing a spread of opportunities in supporting industries. This new exploitation of hidden natural riches, comparable to the opening up of our coal fields in the nineteenth century, has helped us greatly in building the new industrial Scotland. Equally important has been our integration with the stronger English economy, which has given us direct access to the money, skills and markets that make such development possible.

We now, for the first time in many years, have both average earnings and employment levels in Scotland on a par with the rest of the UK. We still of course have plenty of problems. The high level of unemployment brings a degree of frustration and hardship that cannot be accepted and we have still to find ways of making life tolerable in the poorest parts of our society. But we share these problems with other parts of the UK, and indeed of the developed world. Scotland can no longer claim to be a special case, handicapped by inappropriate UK government policies. There will remain more general arguments on the possible benefit to Scotland of following paths of economic policy separate from the UK. These now need to be examined.

Any country or region which has a small population and large industries must expect to sell much of its product abroad. Scotland is no exception. All but the smallest businesses export a large part of their product to England. Scottish business people crowd the air routes to London, not to lobby the government (they can do this better in Edinburgh) but to meet their customers. Trade extends to the European Community, increasingly encouraged by the single market, and overseas. As activities grow, firms set up branch organisations in England and abroad, sometimes new companies which themselves become focuses for international growth. So Scottish industries are networks of transnational relations, operations, and ownership, which they have developed to enable them to produce and trade successfully in the markets of the world. This is no longer confined to the large 'multinationals'. As communication and financial links improve everyone can do it. The little book production firm in Cowdenbeath gets its texts read in Delhi; the baker in Prestonpans opens up in St Petersburg.

Scotland is no different from other industrialised countries or regions in Europe in its international dependence. We have the initial advantage of belonging to an integrated single market, the UK. Beyond that we are part of the developing, but not yet completed, single market of the European Community. Even when that is complete Europe will still look with envy at the example of the USA, where complete integration has brought immense benefits to its component states (Henderson 1992). And there is much more to be done to liberalise trade between the large blocs and the rest of the world. The tortuous and long drawn out GATT negotiations show how difficult it is, once barriers have been built, to break them down again.

The advantages to the citizen, as consumer, of free exchange of goods and services between nations needs no demonstration. The astonishing choice of goods for comfort and satisfaction that we now enjoy is only made possible by a relatively free world trading system. The citizen as producer may be less happy with the uncertainties that this brings. He may lose his job in a Scottish textile factory when his products are undercut by imports from China. There is continual pressure on governments to apply tariffs, at the expense of the European consumer, on those imported products which threaten its home industries. Much of Community policy, instead of promoting free trade, is aimed at preserving the intensely protective structure of the Common Agricultural Policy, at high cost to the citizen and to the developing countries overseas who we claim to support. There are continual adjustments to industrial activity required in every country as demands of consumers change and new or competitive industries grow up inside and outside its boundaries. It is sometimes difficult to accept such adjustments, particularly in times of high unemployment and recession. But it is no remedy to shut out the world and maintain by tariffs high cost and increasingly obsolete industries. In the short term some pain is avoided, but sooner or later the economy sinks. And not only the economy of the first tariff-raising country is sunk, but all those outside whose industries are throttled by the blockage of trade and who have retaliated by similar measures. This is the nightmare scene of the twentieth century, enacted in the slump of the 1930s, and still threatening to appear unless vigorously resisted. The only way to obtain the benefits of free trade with the least possible misery of industrial displacement is to build up a vigorous flexible industrial society where obsolete industries can and will be replaced by new ones to everyone's benefit.

The general acceptance of international free trade as a goal of policy, however much breached in practice, is paralleled by the acceptance of private capitalism, whatever modifying epithets are applied to it, as the engine of prosperity.

There has been a marked change in recent years in political attitudes towards the creation of wealth. Thirty years ago public ownership was still the creed of socialist parties in the democratic world. Soviet Russia was still admired by some as a potential ideal economic society, though flawed. Even Yugoslavia was sometimes held up as a model of successful synthesis of socialism and co-operative capitalism. All this has been swept away. The success of free market capitalist countries, and the dismal failure of central command economies, have left no doubts as to which system can meet the rising demands for material prosperity with respect for the environment. In the newly freed countries of Eastern Europe private property is reinstated, industries are torn out of state ownership, and the joint stock company reappears after fifty years of absence. Even China, last stronghold of Marx and Lenin, has recognised that it will only get the industrial growth it needs by embracing capitalism, turning its southern provinces into a free enterprise park. So in this last decade of the twentieth century we have reached something near to a consensus on economic organisation. This is not entirely a matter of pragmatism. The fires of socialist ideology have died down, but a new ideology has arisen, with Hayek and Adam Smith replacing Marx and Lenin. In industrial terms this calls for free markets and trade, privately owned and voluntarily formed enterprises competing to create and supply markets, rights of citizens as consumers rather than as producers. It is suspicious of government activities. It sees government not as the embodiment of the people's will, but as an instrument of power manipulated and captured by sectional interests, and itself the strongest of interest groups.

This might point to a withering away of the state, a new capitalist Marxism where social and economic interests are so harmonised that governments are no longer necessary. But we have to be less romantic than Marx. We realise that capitalism and free markets, while providing the means to prosperity, do not on their own provide solutions to many of the problems of modern society – sectional poverty, unemployment, security in old age. The job of governments in the future may be more rather than less demanding. They will be relieved of having to run state industries on nebulous criteria of social benefit, and of trying to coerce the wealth-making activities of their millions of citizens into predetermined patterns. But they must ensure that free markets and competition are maintained, and, where they do not or cannot work, look for alternative ways of providing the benefits required.

The movements for Scottish devolution or separation must be judged against this background of national interdependence and the free market ideology which now provides the ground rules for not only Scottish but world business. Scottish businesses are integrated into the UK economy, not just in the absence of trading and currency barriers, but in their network of commercial and personal relationships and in the organisation of their companies. They would aim for the same degree of integration in time with the continent of Europe. It would be totally repugnant to be forced to take steps backwards instead of forwards.

The current proposals for devolution are fluid. During the 1992 election Labour and Liberal Democrats campaigned on the basis of the Scottish Constitutional Convention, which had been endorsed by both parties. Since then the leader of the opposition, initially in an important speech in March 1993, has foreshadowed a complete reform of the constitution of the UK involving parliaments or assemblies not only for Scotland and Wales but also for regions in England. This is a marked change of emphasis. The reform seems likely to follow the outline proposals in the Institute for Public Policy Research pamphlet, *The Constitution of the United Kingdom*. These give parliament (i.e. the UK Parliament) power over matters affecting the freedom of trade and commerce within the UK and trade outside the UK, while responsibility for trade and industry, regional policy and development, transport, energy, agriculture and fisheries is placed with the Assemblies. The overriding power of the UK Parliament on trade and commerce could be interpreted to mean that the economic integration of the whole country would not be affected. Against this there would no doubt be pressure from the Assemblies to obtain independence in control of industrial policy regardless of the overall effect on the UK economy. But the new policy must change devolution prospects considerably, in that many of the separate economic powers claimed by the Constitutional Convention for a devolved Scotland could clearly not be realistically envisaged for a number of regional assemblies that included Scotland and Wales.

Although the Constitutional Convention may now be superseded by this comprehensive scheme for the whole of the UK, it would be useful to set out and examine its provisions. They represent the only detailed policies that have emerged so far at the political level and they still have strong support by devolutionists. A critique of them will also be intended to cover *a fortiori* the economic implications of complete separation as proposed by the Scottish Nationalist Party.

The policies of current devolutionists as set out by the Constitutional Convention (1990) point strongly away from economic integration. They clearly envisage following paths separate from those of the UK government. The proposals of the document include under 'Powers of Scotland's Parliament in the spheres of economic and industrial policy' the following:-

(a) Strategic economic planning powers for industries like whisky, steel, off-shore engineering, food processing, clothing and textiles, agriculture and related land issues, fisheries, some areas of engineering, and possibly electronics and ship-building, where the Scottish industry is not inextricably integrated in the structure of the UK industry.

(b) Powers to co-ordinate the planning of the Scottish components of UK industries where there is a clear inter-relation or where scale demands UK planning. The financial sector, oil and gas, petrochemicals, power and process plant engineering, pharmaceuticals, atomic energy, vehicles, railway policy and aerospace are amongst the most important.

(c) Power via revived and strengthened Scottish Development Agency/Highland and Islands Development Board/Scottish Enterprise to negotiate with multi-nationals over the terms of inward investment within the context of UK regional policy.

(d) Power to initiate some form of public ownership or control in the public interest.

(e) Responsibility for industrial research and development policy with the co-ordinating function in this area for industries with a wider UK base.

(f) Responsibility for monopolies and mergers policy within Scotland. This could mean the establishment of a Scottish Monopolies Commission to act as an effective watch-dog over any attempted takeovers of remaining Scottish companies, or their integration into multi-national operations within the context of UK and EU competition policy.

(g) Power to establish a Scottish international trade organisation, initially with public finance, but which in the long term would be self-financing, to assist in the development of Scottish exports by providing companies with export assistance modelled on the Japanese international trade corporations.

(h) Within the overall context of EU competition and company law, responsibility for the protection of Scottish industry and for company law and registration within Scotland.

(i) Powers to establish Scotland as a competitive and attractive location for companies to establish and to encourage competitive advantage for Scottish-based business.

Some of this represents socialist policies long since discarded by the UK Labour Party, showing the time lag sometimes evident in Scottish political thinking. But, however modified, the industrial policy put forward is intended to differ markedly from that of the UK. Any such divergence would require restrictive controls to fence us off from England. For example, any separate pricing or subsidy policy in particular industries would need protection from England if it made the products more expensive and attract protection by England if it made them cheaper. This would remove the benefits of our present integration and impoverish both countries. The wholly separate Scotland envisaged by the Scottish Nationalists would do this to a much greater degree.

There need be less concern about devolutionist policies for attracting or helping to create new businesses or promote exports. There has been diversity between different regions of UK for many years without upsetting the integrity of the UK economy. Government policies to promote industry in Scotland have borne some fruit. In Scotland we have on the plus side the New Towns and the industry they have attracted, the encouragement of US and Japanese electronic firms to settle here in sufficient concentration to draw ancillary companies to join them. On the minus side there have been spectacular large failures: aluminium in Fort William, the car industry, and some picturesque skeletons in the cupboard of the Highlands and Islands Board and Scottish Development Agency. The underlying mistake was often to plant mature industries in an unsuitable environment, or to establish new industries with insufficient study of marketing and production factors.

It is easy to latch on to the failures and forget the successes. The free market does not provide a limitless supply of entrepreneurs eager to start businesses in the areas where they are wanted. Governments can encourage them by initial development work, infrastructure and modest bribery in the form of grants. We seem to have had some success in doing this in Scotland. Scotland differs from England in having its own development organisations. The Scottish Development Agency, now Scottish Enterprise, has done useful work in promoting and saving medium-size enterprises, getting better at the job over the years. The new Local Enterprise Companies have yet to show whether they can promote industry better on a regional basis.

It is natural that political parties, whether devolutionists or not, looking for solutions to high unemployment, should press for more of this work to be done. But it would be unrealistic to claim that more powers for the existing development agencies, and perhaps some new agencies, would transform Scottish industry. There would probably be diminishing returns from further expansion, and it would certainly be at the expense of other public projects. Any policies for protecting or assisting business adopted by a devolved Scottish Parliament would of course have to remain within limits set by the UK Parliament and indeed by the EU. Both authorities have had to set boundaries to the incentives given to new industry and to the support given to existing industry, both to prevent needless expenditure of public money through the jacking up of competitive offering and to lessen distortion of use of resources.

Spending money to create new industry is attractive to the politician. Established business people are less interested. They gain little from it, and their experience makes them sceptical about the results. But if carefully and skilfully done it must be beneficial, and there should be more voices in favour from those who would benefit, managers of failed businesses which might have been saved, potential future entrepreneurs, and of course the unemployed.

There seems no evidence that promoting new industry would be done any more effectively by a devolved parliament in Edinburgh than, as at present, by the UK Parliament working through the same institutions. Scotland and Wales have to a great extent devised and carried out the policies they wanted within a UK framework.

The most worrying aspect of the Constitutional Convention industrial policy is its protective pessimism. Scottish industry, locked into its past, must be planned, regulated, shielded from takeover, possibly nationalised to preserve it. This suggests a sad stagnation of thought in the political parties concerned. Stability and continuity are desirable ends, but we must accept that if we wish to maintain a high standard of living, and help other countries less favoured than ours to achieve this, industrial stability must give way in many areas to continuous and quite rapid change. Instead of fighting to the last subsidy to preserve declining industries we should be putting all our efforts towards encouraging new industries and providing our people with the skills needed to run them successfully. The emphasis in devolutionist policy is all the other way.

The protectionist attitude is illustrated by the section that would give a Scottish Parliament responsibility for monopolies and merger policies in Scotland and suggests the establishment of a Scottish Monopolies Commission 'to act as an effective watch-dog over any attempted takeovers of remaining (!) Scottish companies' [para. 3(q)]. Though this would be within the context of UK and EU competition policy it is clearly intended that there should be special rules for Scotland. The wording implies that Scotland has a small and fixed number of enterprises which are progressively being taken over by English or other foreign companies. These predators will move Scottish head offices, close down plants and depart with their plunder, leaving Scotland an industrial desert. The picture of a beleaguered citadel, desperately defending its remaining property, is very far from reality. In a living society industrial companies and activities are not static institutions. They are continually changing, some dying, some expanding. New enterprises are continually coming into being. One of the ways by which resources are redeployed is through changes of ownership. Scottish companies buy companies in England as an alternative to building new factories there or to provide a base for expansion. English and overseas companies do the same in Scotland. We must expect this to continue and indeed increase as companies appreciate the benefit of larger operations in the European single market. There is little evidence that mergers and takeovers in Scotland in recent years have harmed our industry overall, and certainly the introduction of overseas companies bringing new industries and skills has been of great benefit.

Behind the very thin economic arguments about protection against takeover there lies a more plausible political case. In an integrated economy such as the UK any region is mathematically likely to have only a small part of its industry owned and controlled within it. Scotland has one tenth of the population of the UK so we might expect to have the same proportion of UK business controlled from Scotland. We should accept this. But because of the centralising attraction of London and south-east England our share is in fact considerably lower than this. There must be some advantage in having more company headquarters in Scotland, bringing an increase in the volume and quality of industrial activity there. Companies often base their research at headquarters, employ high quality corporate staff, and use the services of local lawyers, insurance agents, and accountants. They will probably give some preference in support to local universities, arts companies, and charities. All this has a cumulative effect in attracting and starting new enterprise. Successful regional policy will help to raise the rate of company formation in Scotland and so set more company headquarters here. But government efforts to baptize companies forcibly with a Scottish identity would fail. National distinctions do not fit easily into the pattern of a modern corporation. A Scottish-based company might have a Welsh managing director, two-thirds of its activities in England and another ten per cent overseas, shareholders from London institutions, some of them pension funds ultimately owned by millions of people of every nationality, and bankers from all the countries in which it operates. If it is a good company the directors will have strong loyalties, but they will not be primarily to Scotland. They will be to the company itself, and the groups of people to whom it answers, customers, shareholders, and staff. Nationality will not be a strong factor when decisions are taken to expand operations or close plants, and they will aim to be as good corporate citizens in Munich as they are in Edinburgh. Legislative coercion to force nationality on companies would not work without a battery of statutes so defining and restricting a Scottish company that any self-respecting enterprise with interests outside Scotland would move its registration to Berwick-on-Tweed.

In most of industry nationality of ownership of business is not significant in its effect on the lives of citizens. No one worries that our most successful supermarkets and stores, far ahead of continental countries in the variety of their products and the sophistication of their supply chains, are English. Manufacturing industry has special features. Its factories, particularly under multinational ownership, can be expanded, closed, or moved outside Scotland through decisions taken in London or Tokyo. Scotland, it is feared, could become a low wage country, a 'branch economy', doomed to unskilled assembly jobs, dominated by countries with interests hostile to our own. This is not new or peculiar to Scotland. France had this fear of the Americans twenty years ago. It has now waned. The Americans and Australians have it now of Japan, and they will probably pass through a similar cycle. We might be uncomfortable with foreign owners who were not susceptible to the influence of our government or did not accept the same social responsibilities as other companies. But in the context of the spread of multinational industry and the growing internationalisation of companies themselves this is not a high risk. Companies, wherever their control is based, require to organise their production in the most favourable environments. They will expect to behave in Scotland as well as Scottish companies, or better. They will not be successful if they do not. The transnational corporation has been robustly championed by Henry Wendt (1993), chairman of SmithKline Beecham, who maintains that such companies are more accountable than any other institutions, that their operations spread the highest standards worldwide, and that they encourage cultural diversity by counterweighing the standardising pressures of the nation state. Instead of keeping such companies out, we should welcome all the benefits they can give us, while continually strengthening our education and enterprise base. We can then attract them to upgrade and expand their operations and we can equip our own companies to learn from them and compete with them.

At present UK regulation of mergers and takeovers is through the Office of Fair Trading and the Monopolies Commission. The main criterion is to check market dominance through monopoly power, the line also followed in EU legislation. The commission can consider regional factors and has done so in the past, but not openly in recent years. Much study has been done to consider whether mergers and takeovers benefit economies and to what extent they should be regulated beyond considerations of market dominance, most fully in *Corporate Takeovers and the Public Interest* by Alan Peacock and Graham Bannock (1991). The conclusion has generally been that while the regulatory framework for companies and the stock exchange should be improved to make takeovers for purely financial manipulation more difficult, there would be few occasions outside the established competition criteria on which potential future damage to the economy could justify government intervention to stop a takeover. It does not seem that the Scottish economy has suffered from the narrowing by government policy of the MMC's remit to competitive and market considerations. Peacock and Bannock did not find evidence that external takeovers had damaged industrial activity in Scotland, although the removal of higher decision-making outside Scotland was a cause for concern. Government should certainly keep the right to assess takeovers for the general economic consequences both in regional and in national terms. There could be certain key companies in Scotland – perhaps banks – where a takeover could have damaging effects on economic activity far beyond those on the company itself. Intervention might then be required.

A separate devolved Scottish Commission under a Scottish Parliament would be intended to introduce a much more restrictive policy. The general protection of Scottish industry from outside takeover would damage both the Scottish companies which were stopped from the mergers which shareholders wished to carry through and those which attempted to expand outside Scotland but were frustrated by retaliatory counter measures.

The pattern of restrictive controls or state supports envisaged for industry by the Constitutional Convention is not paralleled in the SNP's policy published in its manifesto of 1992, which concentrates on means of creating new jobs, and does not formulate any specific industrial policy except for steel and fishing, where action through subsidies is proposed. The SNP, in contrast to the Constitutional Convention, is optimistic about Scottish industry and cites its productivity and export performance as a guarantee for Scotland's glowing prospects as a separate state. But it is clear that an independent Scotland would not care about maintaining economic integration with the UK. The essence of independence is the making of separate decisions in industrial policy as elsewhere. It would be surprising if most of the Constitutional Convention requirements were not on the SNP list, though perhaps with a somewhat different political tinge. In any case the adoption of separate currency, banking, and taxation regimes would effectively break the economic integration of the UK, just as they block it in the EU.

We use the language of physical planning and industrial policy in referring to Scotland as a region. In UK terms London is the centre, the seat of government, hub of international trade and finance and site of many of the larger company headquarters. These draw in more population and this itself increases the attraction for industries to set up in the area. So wealth and activity concentrate in London and the south east area of England, leaving the rest of the country, the 'Regions', relatively poor. It has been a prime aim of government policy in the last two generations to counteract the pull of the centre by special regional policies. These policies, as noted above, have had reasonable success. Despite that many Scots have embraced a geographic fatalism. Scotland, they say, is on the periphery of Europe and doomed to be poor. But while there continue to be advantages for industries which settle in more densely populated regions or closer to foreign markets, this is only one factor among many in deciding where industry sets up. Any country or region can develop its own counterbalancing advantages. Finland and Japan are both peripheral on the world map, but neither has found this a handicap. Our governments have applied many types of incentives to encourage new activity and investment in the regions. Scotland has benefited from this as well as from its natural and historical advantages. Any structural and geographical disadvantage of being on the periphery can be best tackled by ensuring that the infrastructure is built up to give economic activity the support it needs. Better, more flexible housing, restoration of crumbling cities, clean up of the wasteland left behind by dead industries, high quality of general and specialist education, good roads, a network of rail and air communication with the south and overseas have all been on the agenda of political parties and have been pursued with some vigour by successive governments, though we will always want more. A devolved Scottish Government would presumably continue with these efforts, but not necessarily more effectively than what is being done at present.

The institutions of government draw to the capital city not only those companies whose prosperity depends on their relations with departures of state, but also financial institutions, trade associations, lobbyists, consultants, think tanks on public policy, and subsidiary government controlled agencies. Government after all spends or transfers between forty or fifty per cent of the yearly wealth that our nation produces. Anyone who is directly concerned in this wants to have close contacts with the seats of power. Decentralising government geographically gives substantial benefits to regions, not only in the activity the dependent institutions bring with them, but also in the social strength they contribute. Government has been quite successful in moving agencies out of London. Some of the quangos have landed in Scotland, e.g. the Forestry Commission and Sea Fish Authority. Civil Service units who carry out the routine jobs of administration have been dispersed throughout the kingdom. Those who make the key policy decisions have stayed firmly in London, and indeed have to be there to work effectively with ministers and colleagues.

We have, of course, our own administration in Edinburgh for the areas for which our Secretary of State is responsible. This would expand somewhat to serve a devolved government, while a separate government would require its own foreign office, defence ministry and treasury as well. But the call for a separate government will need stronger justification than the creation of more government jobs.

Though we are reluctant to admit it, Scotland has enjoyed in recent years a handsome share of UK public expenditure. The figures for public expenditure per head in the UK suggest that we have succeeded in attracting a good deal more than we would get on a strict population basis. This does not suggest that we have been neglected under a UK government. We have indeed had the best of both worlds, a separate administration to argue our case within government and no overall ceiling on our claims. We have secured this, partly because we are more thinly populated than England and so have higher costs for many of the services provided by government, like roads, health and education; partly because we have been one of the poorer areas of the UK and so qualify for regional grants and subsidies. (But we should remember that our relative poverty is not a permanent condition. Up until the 1920s, with our heavy industry supplying the Empire, Scotland was a prosperous place, and in the last few years, as noted above, we have again caught up with the rest of the country.) The main ingredient of our success is perhaps that we exploit to the full our privileged position as a small obstreperous minority within the UK framework. Provided we do not go too far, we can extract concessions out of central government which mean a lot to us but are not large enough to upset the balance of government expenditure.

Part of the public remit for regional subvention has now passed to the EU. The Community administers substantial grants from its programmes to help areas suffering from declining industries, high unemployment or relatively low incomes. Scotland has benefited from this, but as the Community has expanded, with Portugal, Greece and East Germany as new claimants, and previously prosperous areas have been hit by industrial change, it has become more difficult to promote our own claims. The Scottish Office does not have an official presence in Brussels but a number of Scottish public and private bodies have representatives there to gather information and lobby for grants. It is a measure of the crudity and confusion of the EU system that we should need this. It may be necessary, whether or not under devolved government, to have Scottish as well as UK representation at Brussels, if only because other regions in Europe are insisting on this for themselves. But a strong common UK lobby working appropriately for Scottish interests in Community legislation and grants programmes would seem a more effective instrument than separate representation. In some areas where the Scottish interest is predominant, such as fisheries, the Scottish Office might well lead. It would also seem more sensible for the Community to limit itself to dividing the grants between

Member States leaving the states themselves to allocate them in line with Community policy. The UK government in Whitehall and Edinburgh should be better able to judge priorities for regional grants than Brussels, and the money is coming from British taxpayers anyway. The present system with its well-advertised largesse from the EU looks like good publicity for the Community but bad government.

Lobbying represents the pressure put on government by particular interests whether in public or private guise to gain special benefits for themselves, normally at the expense of others. The reconciliation of conflicting claims on its resources is part of the skill of government. But it also exists to promote the general welfare of its citizens, and that may be something quite different from the sum of claims by different interest groups. Modern governments combat this by renouncing responsibility as much as possible for detailed economic activity. But a large amount remains under its control. The smaller the unit of government the greater the danger that strong interests may capture parts of it to their own advantage, and to the prejudice of the citizen, whether large companies, trade unions, or associations promoting particular public causes. This is the reverse side of the sensitivity to public opinion which ought to be one of the merits of smaller government units. It does not make a good reason for rejecting devolution. But it must be marked on the debit side. In a healthy economic culture businesses will want their prosperity to depend on their success in finding and satisfying customers, not on the lobbying of government for favours.

There is a more general message here. Mancur Olson (1982) has argued convincingly that the economic success of countries relates to their ability to curb the self-preserving influence of special interest organisations such as industries, unions or professions. This further suggests that the more interest groups, in the shape of regions, are given their head in the political systems of the Community, the more the economic advantages of growing economic integration will be postponed.

Taxation is a sensitive issue in any debate on devolution. The more an economy is integrated with its neighbours the less scope it has for varying tax rates. This is already becoming evident in the countries of the EU, linked by free trade but still far from integrated. In Scotland even a small increase in the company tax rate would nudge companies towards making their domicile elsewhere. With individual taxation the results would not be so immediate, but a higher rate would hasten the flow of talented Scots over the border and lessen our recruitment of talented non-Scots, both to our loss. The Constitutional Convention proposed to give power to a parliament to vary income tax up or down but within a defined range. Ten per cent was discussed as a limit. Even such an apparently small variation applied upwards would have its effect.

Taxation to finance local government could in principle be decided separately by a devolved government. Local authorities already have freedom to set their own rates and these have varied considerably. Differences in local taxation do not provoke the same reaction as differences in income or corporation tax. They are a smaller part of taxation and, while individuals can move house, factories and shops cannot easily be put elsewhere. In practice local freedom to tax was always supplemented by equalisation grants. Both the business rating system and the old house rating system have now broken down. Business rates in Scotland have over the years moved to an intolerable level, far higher than England, mainly due to the insensitivity of Scottish local authorities. The fiasco of attempting to replace property tax by poll tax showed, not so much that people will not pay taxes that they think unfair, but that they resent paying any tax at all that is not deducted at source by employer or shop-keeper. We currently have business rates that are moving to become uniform throughout the UK, a property tax not far from the original that was abandoned, and local government mostly financed by central taxation. It has been an axiom of local government that councils should be responsible to their electors in both raising and spending money. The link, at best weak and incomplete, is now quite broken. If local government is to carry out the functions for which it is suited a new more robust system must be thought out. This does not need to be uniform between Scotland and England. But a generally higher local tax level for Scotland would in the longer term discourage industry from Scotland.

We are fortunate in having in Scotland already a high degree of devolution in the departments and organisations serving industry. Those responsible know their clients and their problems far better than their opposite numbers in England trying to cover ten times as much. Standards are high. Civil servants involved in industry have largely been creative and effective in their jobs, though their achievements, following the admirable tradition of anonymity, have been unsung. The quangoes, in whose hands rests much of the administration of the country, have been progressively devolved. In the past two years, for instance, Scottish Heritage and the Scottish Higher Education Funding Council have come into being, step children of Nature Conservancy and the University Funding Council. Sometimes the relations between such Scottish quangos and their UK counterparts cause friction but usually they come to a working agreement which leave Scottish quangos free to follow their own paths while conforming to UK policy.

As has been pointed out, it would be an easy change to make the present Scottish departments of government responsible not only to Scottish ministers, as they already are, but to a Scottish Parliament. It can be claimed that without a separate parliament there is a 'democratic deficiency' in the supervision of the Scottish ministers and their departments. Democratic control is at present supplied by the Westminster Parliament, with Scottish MP's closely involved. A move to an Edinburgh Parliament of these functions would certainly allow more control, though with the threat to underlying unity of policies diverged.

Government in the 1990s will be increasingly involved in means and less in ends. It is becoming of high importance that the delivery of public services should be singleminded and effective. One of the main drives of government over the past ten years has been to organise these services better to meet the needs of the citizens who use them. Privatisation, contracting out to independent agencies, and provision of cost and price structures to guide allocation of resources have been introduced. This has to be pursued with determination, otherwise there is no prospect of the public sector being able to maintain in the future the responsibilities it has been allotted, while industry and individuals will collapse under the weight of taxation. The work of new quangoid structures will, to the extent that they cannot be regulated by markets, no doubt continue to be reported to parliament through the departments and ministers concerned, and a widely spread membership of the boards and committees concerned will give some degree of democratic control. More direct accountability will probably be required. A Scottish Parliament could help here, holding periodic reviews of Scottish institutions. But a better formula may well be the restoration of the powers and prestige of local government through stronger single tier authorities, coupled with greater responsibilities for the Scottish committees of the UK Parliament working in Westminster and Edinburgh. The proposals of the 'stocktaking' White Paper of March 1993 (Scottish Office 1993) move in this direction. The dangers for Scottish industry are that such a new parliament, interested primarily in national self-assertion, would not long remain satisfied with a limited watch-dog role. Regardless of the initial constitution it would soon want to move the balance of powers away from the UK, and would feel frustrated if this was denied. There would then be progressive steps towards breaking the integration which we have enjoyed so long. Intervention to promote Scottish industrial interests at the expense of the rest of the UK, whatever its immediate attractions, would soon damage us badly by restricting us and cutting away our markets.

It is unfortunate that the devolution debate has been driven by the political balance of parties in Scotland. It is natural that the Labour Party in Scotland, overwhelmingly in the majority, should feel frustrated that it is unable to carry out its policies there. Similarly the Liberal Democrats can see more influence coming their way in a Scottish Parliament, elected by proportional representation, than they can muster at Westminster. On the other side Scottish businesses, who have past experience of the hostility of Labour-controlled local authorities to private industry, expect that a Labour-controlled parliament would turn the clock back against private enterprise. They feel it would strengthen also the present fiefdoms of local government and the entrenched interests that surround it. Some of these fears are out-dated. Scottish local government is getting more comfortable and co-operative in working with business to solve industrial problems. But the worry remains.

Any devolution proposals must take some account of the current difference in majority political opinion between Scotland and England. But this cannot be the dominating factor in deciding for a Scottish Parliament. Political opinion changes. Quite a small further swing away from the Tories would have brought Labour to power in 1992. The devolution movement would then have lost much of its steam. Nor is it inevitable that Labour should hold a permanent majority of votes in Scotland. If this was eroded there might be much less political enthusiasm for devolution. The main yardsticks for devolution should be those of good government and democracy. A large part of good government is the promotion of material prosperity. The arguments of this essay have suggested that a Scottish Parliament would be at best irrelevant, at worst harmful, to this aim.

We should always remember that advances in government, as in the creation of wealth, are made by widening circles of co-operation over the barriers of geography, history and culture. The broadening of government, on the principle of sharing, not segregating, power, and the corresponding extension of free trade and markets, must remain a worthy ideal, to be pursued as much in the UK, where we take it for granted, as in Europe and internationally. Our democracy has worked well over the past hundred years. The rule of majority has been historically tempered, as it must be, by accommodation of minorities whether political, economic, or cultural. Scotland has maintained its traditional institutions within the Union, and on the rare occasions when it has urged a coherent national view this has been respected. Some Scots will maintain that this is not enough. But it would be sad if their narrowing visions were allowed to turn us from the liberal paths of economic progress.

Constitutional Change and the Scottish Financial Sector

Andrew Bain

Introduction

Scotland has a worldwide reputation for sound and astute financial management. It has its own banking system, life assurance companies which supply 20% of the UK market, and investment management companies which compete effectively in both UK and international markets. In terms of the equity funds under management Scotland ranks as the fourth largest centre in the EU. The significance of the financial sector for the Scottish economy therefore lies not only in the financial services provided within Scotland, but also more importantly in the business it brings to Scotland – it is a major service export industry.

The *size* of the Scottish financial sector – its contribution to Scotland's GDP and employment – depends on what is regarded as 'financial' business. The broadest definition covers banking, finance and business services (Division 8 of the 1980 Standard Industrial Classification), which accounted for about 10% of employment – 198,000 employees – in 1991. However, within this total about 50% were employed in 'business services', a category which includes inter alia accountants, advertising executives, architects, estate agents, consulting engineers, lawyers and private detectives, most of whom are not engaged primarily in activities concerned with the provision or management of finance; and another 14% or so are involved in hiring out moveable equipment, for example cars, television sets, and construction equipment, or in the ownership or management of real estate. The estimated 'contribution' of this broad sector to GDP was 14%, though little attention should be paid to this measure, which is artificial and exaggerates the sector's importance.

In this chapter I shall therefore treat the financial sector as a more narrowly defined *financial services* sector, corresponding to the financial intermediation sector in the 1992 Standard Industrial Classification, and consisting of banking, other financial institutions, insurance and activities auxiliary to these sectors. Employment in these financial services in September 1991 amounted to 77,000, about 4% of Scotland's total, having risen from 60,000 a decade earlier. Employment incomes are probably a little above the average for the whole economy, in spite of relatively high proportions of part-time female employees in some parts of the sector, so the financial sector accounts for perhaps 5% of employment incomes.

While some of the other business services in the more broadly defined sector make significant inputs to the financial intermediation sectors amongst others, they are better regarded as suppliers to the sector than as part of it.

Employment income is probably the best measure of the financial service sector's *direct* contribution to the Scottish economy, but there are also important indirect contributions. The sector makes substantial demands on the outputs of other sectors as inputs to its own activities; and leading figures from the financial sector often fulfil a leadership role in society at large, with the financial institutions acting as sponsors of sporting events, supporters of the arts, and donors of funds for major projects in Scotland.

In analysing the probable effects of constitutional change on the Scottish financial sector, it is important to distinguish between Scottish-based institutions which seek to serve a wider market; servicing functions located in Scotland of businesses which are head-quartered elsewhere; and organisations located in Scotland in order to serve customers who are also in Scotland. The effects of any constitutional changes on their costs is significant for all these groups, but for the first there are also crucial marketing factors to be taken into account, and for the second there are issues connected with nationality: for a UK company, a decision to site a servicing organisation in, say, the Republic of Ireland is materially different from deciding to locate it in Wales, Yorkshire or Scotland.

The Scottish Financial Sector

The Scottish financial sector can usefully be divided into the following segments:

> clearing banks, merchant banks, and building societies;
> insurance companies;
> investment managers;
> stock-market and related services;
> miscellaneous specialised organisations.

The banks

In terms of their total assets – nearly £75 billion at the end of January 1993 – the four Scottish Clearing Banks (Bank of Scotland, Clydesdale Bank, The Royal Bank of Scotland and TSB Scotland) dominate this category. They provide all the usual banking services within Scotland, but in addition two – Bank of Scotland and The Royal Bank of Scotland – are also heavily involved in England and Wales. For the Bank of Scotland this business is done through a number of corporate branches in key locations in England and through a subsidiary company, the Bank of Wales, while The Royal operates through a wider branch network developed from the former Williams and Glyns bank which was merged into The Royal Bank. Both have been expanding their share of banking business outside Scotland in recent years – the opportunities to expand market share are much greater than in Scotland where they are already dominant. Clydesdale, which along with Yorkshire Bank in England and Northern Bank in Ulster is owned by National Australia Bank, concentrates much more heavily on business in Scotland, and TSB Scotland is responsible for the Scottish operations of the TSB Group.

All the Clearers other than TSB Scotland maintain London offices for Treasury and related money-market and foreign exchange business, as well as other commercial lending. No distinction is drawn between Scottish and English business – deposits go into and loans are drawn from a common pool; liquidity and capital requirements are judged by reference to their business as a whole.

Bank of Scotland owns The British Linen Bank, its merchant banking subsidiary with headquarters in Edinburgh, and NWS Bank, a finance and leasing company based in Chester. The Royal Bank sold its merchant banking subsidiary, Charterhouse Bank, in 1993. It has a growing involvement in insurance business, partly through its Direct Line insurance subsidiary, which has been gaining market share throughout the UK and has expanded its processing facilities in Glasgow, and partly through a joint venture life assurance company with the Scottish Equitable Life Assurance Society. Both banks have interests in fund management, through Dunedin Investment Management and Capital House Investment Management respectively. The former is based in Edinburgh, while the latter is divided between London and Edinburgh – fund management in London, processing and some other operations in Edinburgh. TSB Scotland provides similar services in Scotland through associated Group companies – the central mortgage processing facility for the TSB Group is situated in Glasgow.

The Royal Bank and the Bank of Scotland are also involved in activities outside the UK, the former to a greater extent than the latter. For The Royal the most important are its ownership of Citizens Financial Group in the US and its link with Banco Santander in Spain, though it also has less significant trade investments in a number of other countries. Bank of Scotland's international activities are less extensive – it owns Countrywide Banking Corporation Limited in New Zealand, and participates in joint ventures in Germany and Italy.

Thus while Clydesdale's and TSB Scotland's activities are mainly directed towards the domestic Scottish market, both Bank of Scotland and The Royal Bank have the character of financial groups based in Scotland but serving elements of the UK market as a whole, and also having significant international interests. The head office activities connected with all these operations generate income and employment in Scotland, as do the Direct Line and TSB Group mortgage activities located in Scotland.

There are five Scottish merchant banks, of which The British Linen Bank is much the largest. While the merchant banks are particularly concerned with corporate finance and other activities in Scotland, they are also involved to a greater or lesser degree with business in the rest of the UK and sometimes overseas. Again, their contribution to economic activity in Scotland reflects the range of their business. The domestic Scottish market is also served by several branches or subsidiaries of merchant banks and venture capital companies based in London, as well as by a number of corporate finance companies.

The only substantial building society based in Scotland is the Dunfermline Building Society, whose retail deposit-taking and lending operations are almost entirely within Scotland. Like other building societies, its liquid assets are invested in, and wholesale funds obtained from, UK markets. The greater part of building society business in Scotland is, however, carried out by English societies through their extensive Scottish branch networks. Deposit-taking and lending in Scotland are integrated with their activities in the rest of the UK. Thus, as with the banks, deposits go into and loans are drawn from a common pool of sterling funds.

Insurance

There are ten Scottish life offices, with over 14,000 employees in Scotland. Their combined share of the UK market in long-term life assurance and pensions is 20%. Five are mutual offices based in Scotland; the others are proprietary companies run from Scotland but which are subsidiaries of other organisations. Three – Abbey National Life, Britannia Life, and Royal Scottish – are 'bancassurers' which make use of the bank or building society branches of their parent bodies to sell their products. Standard Life, the largest mutual life assurance office in Europe, has extensive interests in Canada, several companies have long-standing interests in the Republic of Ireland, and some have or are in the process of establishing operations in other European countries. Their funds – over £90 billion at the end of 1993 – are invested in UK and international capital markets.

In essence the life offices sell long-term savings products, operating in an extremely competitive market. Some 90% of their UK business emanates from outside Scotland. They have basically three methods of marketing their products – through their own sales forces, through independent advisers, and through tied agents. In recent years, thanks to competitive developments in the financial services industries generally and to the provisions of the Financial Services Act 1986 in particular, there has been a strong trend away from independent advisers and towards tied agents and bancassurers.

Success in gaining new business is dependent on the quality of service provided to advisers and agents, the level of operating costs, and above all investment performance and reputation. Financial advisers must have confidence in the offices with which they place their clients' long-term savings. The same goes for other organisations, such as building societies bringing a flow of mortgage-related business, which will not be prepared to form a link with an insurance company unless they have confidence in its future performance. A key consideration for the life assurance companies is therefore the effect of any constitutional change on the perceptions of advisers and agents, as well as of potential policy-holders, in so far as any change in these perceptions may affect their ability to win new business in their markets.

General Accident, the third largest general insurer in the UK, is the only major composite insurance company based in Scotland. It undertakes worldwide business, with very substantial interests in the UK and North America. Its headquarters and main administrative centre are in Perth, with an operations centre also recently set up in Dundee; the life assurance component of its business is run from York.

Compared with life insurance, general insurance is short-term in nature. Reputation, e.g. for dealing with brokers and settling claims efficiently, is very important, but contracts are normally renewed annually – unlike savings products, the long-term investment performance is not an issue for the client. Any effects of constitutional change on operating costs are therefore likely to be of greater importance than effects on market reputation or image.

Investment fund management

One of the most notable distinctive characteristics of the Scottish financial sector is its strength in equity fund management. As already noted, this is a prime activity of the life assurance offices, who are responsible for the greater part of the funds, but in addition there are a number of major independent fund managers dealing with investment trusts, unit trusts, segregated funds such as pension and charitable funds, and private clients. The total funds under management were about £45 billion at the end of 1993, including about a third of the investment trust assets in the UK. The position of the Scottish fund managers in the segregated UK pension funds market is much weaker, where there has been a tendency for business to gravitate towards a small number of much larger, London-based institutions, and the Scottish institutions were relatively late entrants to unit trust business.

In practically all of their business the fund managers face intense competition in the UK or international markets. The key factor for competitive success is, of course, investment performance, and this depends primarily on their ability to attract and retain specialist staff of the necessary quality. But they are also helped in marketing their services by the generally high reputation and favourable image of Scottish financial institutions, and by the relatively low cost base for non-specialist activities enjoyed by efficient organisations in Scotland. Any effects of constitutional change on their staffing, costs or image would have implications for their business.

Stock market and related services

Members of the Scottish unit of the Stock Exchange provide advisory, portfolio management and stock exchange dealing services to clients in Scotland and, particularly in the case of shares in Scottish registered companies, elsewhere. They also act as official brokers to companies. The larger firms of stockbrokers are now part of wider-ranging groups, with the Scottish offices providing important services to the group as a whole as well as being responsible for local business. Allied Provincial Securities has its headquarters in

Glasgow, and a significant part of NatWest Securities Limited's research function is located in Edinburgh. In addition, all the settlements for business carried out through Barclays Bank are handled in Scotland. As a result, the exchange in Glasgow handles 50% of the settlements in the UK retail market and almost 20% of overall UK business.

These 'back-office' activities can now be carried out quite separately from the 'front-office' activities to which they relate. Their presence in Scotland reflects the fact that it is a cost-effective location for them. There is still considerable scope for firms in London and elsewhere to shift back-office work to lower-cost centres or to buy in settlement services. Any effects of constitutional change on Scotland's ability to win this business will therefore be important.

Specialised services

Scotland is home of a number of specialised service companies and organisations, developed in some cases from other financial businesses. The largest is The WM Company, which spun out of stockbrokers Wood Mackenzie, now part of NatWest Securities, and which employs over 400 qualified staff. It provides accounting, valuation and performance measurement services to other fund managers in 20 countries. It is an autonomous subsidiary of Bankers Trust Company, which runs its European Global Custody service from the same premises. Another example is Save and Prosper Group's investment administration service, employing over 70 people. For these businesses the quality of communications is a key consideration, and constitutional arrangements are relevant mainly in so far as they might influence operating costs.

In the public sector the National Savings Bank and the Student Loans Company, both located in Glasgow, carry out the administration in their respective fields for the whole of the UK. Any constitutional changes which affected the integrity of the UK would call in question their continued location in Scotland.

The Effects of Constitutional Change

In considering the effects of constitutional change on the Scottish financial sector, it is helpful to distinguish between *permanent* effects associated with either full independence or a devolved structure of government, and a number of important *transitional* effects which might occur both during the period leading up to the constitutional change and afterwards as a consequence of the change itself.

A fully independent Scotland would have its own currency (unless it participated in an EU monetary union), its own arrangements for supervising financial institutions, its own taxes on individuals and companies, and its own labour and other laws affecting the operating conditions of companies in Scotland. Its government would be free to pursue the economic policies of its choice, subject however to the constraints imposed by international competition and obligations such as membership of the EU. These attributes of independence would result in permanent changes in the business environment for Scottish financial institutions. There would in addition be a number of important temporary or transitional effects as a result of the process of introducing a new currency and the absence initially of any track record for a new Scottish Government.

The permanent effects of devolution for Scotland would depend on the powers which were devolved, and the political context in which the devolution took place. Proposals for a devolved structure of government for Scotland might generate considerable resentment, affecting the image of Scottish finance in other UK markets. Moreover, prior to any constitutional change there would inevitably be considerable uncertainty about the nature of the new structure to be created and the policies which any new administration would adopt. These effects – temporary or permanent – of devolution could have important consequences for the business of Scottish financial institutions.

An independent Scotland

The introduction of an independent Scottish currency would give rise to major transitional problems for the financial sector, particularly the banks and life assurance companies, all stemming from the possibility that the exchange rate between sterling and the Scottish currency might change. Even if a Scottish Government declared its intention to maintain the parity with sterling, in the conditions likely to prevail in the foreseeable future no-one could be certain that it would not act differently; there would be perceived to be a risk that the exhange rate would change. Membership of an EU-wide monetary union (including sterling) would, of course, overcome this difficulty, but no such monetary union is in sight.

In the process of introducing an independent currency it would be necessary to divide all the banks' monetary assets and liabilities into two categories – those which continued to be fixed in sterling and those which were converted into Scottish currency. Precisely how this was done would, of course, depend on legislation passed by a Scottish Parliament. Presumably bank deposits held in Scotland by Scottish residents would be eligible for conversion into Scottish currency obligations, as would loans to Scottish residents. But what of residents' deposits – often substantial – with English offices of Scottish banks, non-residents' deposits with Scottish offices of all banks, and Scottish banks' loans to non-residents? The situation would clearly be complex – perhaps *all* depositors and borrowers would have to be given the choice of retaining their sterling obligations or converting them into obligations denominated in Scottish currency.

For the banks, simply identifying deposit and loan balances as either sterling or Scottish currency could not be the end of the story, for as soon as the exchange rate between sterling and Scottish currency could conceivably vary they could no longer treat their funds as belonging to a single pool: each bank's total sterling assets would have to be broadly matched against their sterling liabilities and their Scottish currency assets against their Scottish currency liabilities, since otherwise the bank would be exposed to an unacceptable risk of gain or loss if the exchange rate changed. Banks operating in Scotland would have to manipulate deposit and loan interest rates to achieve the required balance. For example, if there was a shortage of Scottish-currency deposits initially, both deposit and loan rates of interest would need to be raised. This could easily occur initially if Scottish depositors chose to retain a substantial proportion of their existing deposits in sterling rather than take the risk of holding deposits denominated entirely in a new and untried currency. Building societies would be subject to the same pressures as the banks.

These problems would almost certainly cause considerable disruption in the run-up to and years immediately following independence. When overall balance between Scottish currency assets and liabilities had been achieved, individual banks and building societies could eliminate any remaining imbalances in their own positions through an interbank market, and after independence any overall imbalance could in principle be alleviated by a new Scottish Central Bank and by the development of new markets in Scottish-currency denominated assets. All this would take time. However, these adverse consequences of independence would not be permanent. For both the banks and their customers, permanent effects would result only from the need to work with assets denominated in two currencies and the costs involved in hedging the resulting exchange rate risks.

The introduction of a new currency would also give rise to major transitional problems for the life assurance companies. To convert all the policies issued by Scottish life offices into Scottish currency obligations would be unacceptable to those policy-holders – the great majority – who do not reside in Scotland, so that in practice, conversion would have to be confined to policies held by Scottish residents. Even then conversion would probably take place only with the agreement of the policy-holder – if conversion for Scottish residents was made compulsory many Scottish policy-holders would acquire accommodation addresses in England or elsewhere! Thereafter, in managing their funds, the life companies would have to take account of the currency composition of their liabilities.

The arrangements for supervising financial institutions, to ensure inter alia that banks are able to repay deposits, that insurance companies do not default on their obligations to policy-holders and that pension funds' managers do not walk off with the pension schemes' funds, would be a further cause of difficulty for the Scottish financial sector. Following current EU practice, an independent Scotland would be responsible for the prudential supervision of its own financial institutions. No supervisory authorities for this purpose exist in Scotland at present, and new regulations and institutions would have to be created, or perhaps brought in for a transitional period. While in one respect this could be advantageous to Scottish institutions, since it is arguable that in some areas the present UK arrangements are unduly burdensome and costly, in other respects the Scottish banks, life offices and fund managers would be liable to lose out.

The source of the problems for the Scottish banks would be that depositors, other banks with which they deal, and international credit rating agencies might reasonably have more confidence in supervisory authorities with experience and a track record than with new, untested organisations, amd that as a result the banks' access to deposits would be impaired. For the major banks the most likely adverse consequences would be a slight increase in the cost of funds and a weakening in their competitive position outside Scotland. But the effects on the smaller banks could be much more severe. Though the effects would diminish with time when the effectiveness of the supervisory arrangements in Scotland had been established, part could well be permanent.

For the life assurance companies the result of changing to supervision by a 'foreign' agency could be very serious. The crucial importance of advisers and agents having confidence in the life office with which business is placed has already been stressed. There is little international business in life assurance, and advisers or agents in England (standing henceforth for the rest of the UK) would have to justify recommending clients to place business with a foreign company rather than with an English company offering comparable policies. Thus the uncertainty created by different supervisory arrangements – the risk that a client would have a claim against them if a foreign life office defaulted on its obligations or performed unsatisfactorily – could easily lead advisers to recommend clients to place their business elsewhere and agents to discontinue their existing links with Scottish life offices. The most probable result for the Scottish life offices would be a considerable loss of new business in their most important market.

If in the course of time the EU becomes a single market for life assurance, with cross-border business becoming as common as domestic business is now, these considerations will disappear. But that is a prospect for the future, not the reality today. For practical purposes the potential damage to the life offices can therefore be regarded as permanent.

Independent fund managers might expect to encounter similar difficulties in the segregated pension fund market. Whereas most of the 'international' business won by Scottish fund managers has been for specialised components of larger portfolios, in the UK they can expect to manage all or a substantial part of a core portfolio. Trustees in England might well be reluctant to entrust the management of all or substantial parts of their funds to managers who were no longer subject to the English supervisory authorities.

The tax arrangements specifically applicable to financial institutions could be a further source of difficulty for the Scottish financial sector, though in the long-run the opposite is also possible. It is by no means inconceivable that a Scottish Government would enact legislation which placed the Scottish financial institutions in a favourable position in comparison with competitors in other countries. Some supporters of independence advocate such a policy, in order to give financial institutions in Scotland the advantages of Luxembourg or an offshore financial centre. If this did happen, and was expected to persist, Scottish institutions would enjoy the benefits.

But it is not at all certain that it would happen, and regardless of the eventual outcome, the risk of disadvantageous tax treatment would create temporary difficulties for the Scottish financial sector.

For the banks, the tax treatment of interest payments would be a matter of particular concern. At present, for private individuals, banks withhold income tax at the standard rate unless the individual is a non-taxpayer. Interest to non-residents of the UK is paid without any deduction for tax. If, after independence, residents of Scotland and England were accorded non-resident status by bank offices in the other country, the result would be massive cross-border flows of funds in both directions, the scale depending, no doubt, on the degree of co-operation between tax authorities which was thought likely. Any differences in withholding taxes according to the status of the depositor would have similar effects, though to a lesser degree.

The taxation of life funds is complex, with rates bearing some relation to the income taxes payable by individuals. It is possible that Scottish legislation would mirror English, but there is a risk that it would not do so (particularly if income tax rates in Scotland were higher than in England) and that the life funds of the Scottish offices would thus be taxed more heavily than their English counterparts with unavoidable adverse consequences for the benefits paid out in future years. Again, even if this is thought unlikely it is not something that a financial adviser, agent, or potential policy-holder in England could discount altogether. The safe course of action would be to place business with English life offices, at least until a Scottish government had acquired a satisfactory track record. However, similar arguments are not applicable to segregated funds, such as pension funds managed on behalf of English companies, which would normally be taxed under the arrangements applying to funds in their own country.

For the life offices the risk of a substantial loss of new business as a result of independence is therefore serious, and it is not a threat which they could afford to ignore. It could, however, be avoided altogether by shifting their country of incorporation to England. Since they are all heavily dependent on business from outside Scotland, this would be a rational response. Moving their brass plates to England would not necessarily entail a similar move in the location of their staff and activities, but to ensure that they came under English regulatory jurisdiction the effective control of the business would need to be located in England; i.e. some of the highest level functions in the company would have to be moved to England. It would not be necessary to move to London – Leeds and Manchester could offer supporting financial expertise and cost levels which are comparable to those available in Scotland. But inevitably, once top management had gone, there would be a tendency for the proportion of activities conducted from England to increase gradually thereafter.

Independence would also call in question the continued presence in Scotland of the National Savings Bank and Student Loans Company. In due course these could be expected to migrate south, leaving only operations suited to the need of their Scottish customers. However, there would be some offset to this loss of employment as activities carried out in England for Scottish customers migrated back to Scotland, and both a Scottish Central Bank and supervisory organisations for the financial sector would provide new sources of employment in Scotland.

The fact that Scotland had become a foreign country would also be likely to affect inward investment by UK private sector organisations. The migration of back-office operations from London to relatively low cost locations in Scotland would be likely to suffer. As noted earlier, for companies based in the rest of the UK moving operations to another country is qualitatively different to moving them elsewhere in the UK. Whereas today Scotland is competing on an equal footing with other locations in the UK (sometimes with an advantage thanks to regional grants and other incentives) for this kind of business, an independent Scotland would be at a disadvantage. As regards inward investment from other countries, however, Scotland's international competitive position would be unlikely to be affected materially by independence, except in so far as domestic operating cost levels might be influenced.

The effect which independence would have on financial institutions' operating costs is a key issue for the financial sector – indeed for those parts of the sector where independence would have little permanent effect on the marketing of their services, such as the fund managers, the effect on operating costs is *the* key issue. The operating costs of financial institutions would be affected by wage and salary levels, by taxes and social security contributions levied on business, by employment laws and by all the other factors (such as planning regulations) which affect the ease with which business can operate in a country.

It is not possible to say whether wages generally (including social security costs) would be higher or lower as a result of independence -presumably in the end real wage costs would have to move to a level which allowed the Scottish economy as a whole to be competitive in world markets, if necessary through an adjustment of the exchange rate for the Scottish currency. The overall level of taxes and social security contributions would be determined by public expenditure in Scotland. Again it is not easy to predict how these would change, though in view of the political complexion of Scotland it does not seem likely that they would be lower than in England. However, the need to attract firms to Scotland and retain existing firms makes it unlikely that taxes on profits would be set above the English level. Some convergence of the costs imposed by labour laws in EU countries is probable, though it is possible that an independent Scotland would implement the Social Chapter of the Maastricht Treaty ahead of England. Other business costs should not be materially affected.

The level of personal taxation would have important implications for operating costs in some of the financial institutions, particularly those which employ highly mobile, qualified personnel whose earnings are subject to higher rates of tax. Fund managers estimate that about 70% of their staff costs are for employees in this category – employees who choose to work in Scotland, but who, in many cases, could and often have worked in England or abroad. To retain their services firms in Scotland have to pay salaries which provide them with an acceptable standard of living when seen in comparison with opportunities elsewhere. This means in effect that differences in tax rates between countries have eventually to be reflected in differences in gross salaries, so that net incomes are unaffected.

High taxes add to business costs because gross salaries have to be set at higher levels to provide the same net income. This is a familiar situation for multinational firms, which are accustomed to taking account of tax levels in determining the salaries to be paid to staff in different countries. Many firms in the financial sector employ an above average proportion of people affected by these considerations, and the competitive position of the Scottish financial sector depends crucially on firms' ability to attract and retain these highly-paid people.

Even if marginal tax rates in an independent Scotland turned out to be no higher than in England, so that there was no permanent addition to operating costs from this source, the fear that such taxes might be levied could easily discourage prospective employees from accepting posts in Scotland in the years surrounding a move to independence. Potential employees would judge that, while market forces would eventually compel firms to compensate their mobile employees for higher taxes, in the short term it would be the employees themselves who had to bear the greater part of the burden.

Thus the possibility of higher marginal taxes on income would be liable to add to some of the financial institutions' operating costs or reduce their effectiveness in the transitional period surrounding independence. Whether costs were raised permanently would depend on the policies which a Scottish Government pursued.

Supporters of independence frequently assert that it would in itself act as a catalyst for change in the Scottish economy, stimulating entrepreneurship and raising efficiency generally. To the extent that this occurred the financial sector, along with others, would benefit from an improvement in the business climate which could easily outweigh the effects of any permanent increases in operating costs due to other factors. However, such long-run benefits are conjectural, and the expectation of temporary increases in costs until these long-run benefits had come through would remain.

In view of the discussion above it is hardly surprising that most of the financial institutions see independence as a considerable threat to their future prosperity. While the likelihood of permanent effects on their costs is doubtful the threat of permanent damage to many of the major institutions' access to the English market is palpable. There would also be major transitional problems affecting both costs and market access adversely. Moreover, while some components of the sector would be affected much more severely than others, all elements benefit from the strength of the sector as a whole, so that, for example, any major weakening in life assurance would have adverse repercussions on fund management and security services generally in Scotland.

Devolution

The consequences of devolution for the financial sector would depend on the nature of the devolved structure and powers devolved, the perceived stability of that structure, and the political context within which devolution took place.

The maintenance of an integrated UK market for financial products is a prime concern for many major Scottish financial institutions. This will be achieved only if financial institutions are subject to common supervisory regimes and tax treatment of their funds throughout the UK. There have been no proposals that these powers should be devolved to a Scottish administration, and under devolution the creation of a separate Scottish currency, which would also fragment the economy, is not an issue. Nor would devolution be likely to lead to any distinctive labour legislation in Scotland.

If, as has been proposed, a Scottish administration had the power to vary income tax levels, this could affect the competitive position of Scottish financial institutions (favourably or unfavourably). As noted above, to the extent that they are not matched by compensating differences in benefits, regional tax differences can be expected to feed through eventually into the wages and salaries paid to mobile staff, with consequences for operating costs. It is also likely that the cost of some supplies would be affected. However, provided that tax rates could be varied only within narrow limits, the long-run effects of any differences should not be exaggerated – other differences in local taxation do not have a major impact.

It follows that a devolved structure per se need not necessarily have any significant positive or negative effects on the Scottish financial sector – hardly a surprise, since financial institutions operate effectively in regional centres in other countries with much less centralised political structures than that of the UK. If a devolved or less centralised structure provided cheaper and more effective administration generally, financial institutions, like other sectors, would stand to benefit. And if a Scottish administration pursued policies which raised business costs relative to those in other regions, businesses in Scotland would suffer a competitive disadvantage.

The prosperity of the Scottish financial sector need not therefore be much affected, either favourably or adversely, by the fact of devolved government. It could, however, be seriously affected by the political context in which a more devolved system of government was introduced. The issues here concern the stability of the devolved structure – would it be seen as a step on the road to full independence? – and on any resentment against the Scots which a move towards greater devolution might create.

If the devolved structure was perceived as unstable, the uncertainties associated with independence would come into play. If Scotland were to become independent, how would life assurance funds be taxed, would existing policies be compulsorily converted into a new currency, would there be new arrangements for supervision, would people working in Scotland be taxed more heavily, and so on? All the negative consequences of independence for the financial institutions' business would emerge to some degree, with none of the possible compensating benefits which might conceivably result from full independence.

If, in addition, devolution was introduced reluctantly in response to intense political pressure from Scotland, whilst the influence of Scottish Members of Parliament over decisions affecting England was retained, it would inevitably give rise to resentment against the Scots. The (presently very favourable) image of Scottish institutions as suppliers of financial services in England would suffer – with adverse consequences not only for the banks and life assurance companies but also for the fund management groups. Resentment against Scotland would also be a factor tipping the balance in inward investment decisions.

The perceived stability of devolved government in Scotland would, of course, be influenced by the political context in which it was introduced. A fiercely contested special deal for the Scots would not be perceived as permanent. However, if devolution for Scotland were introduced in the context of greater devolution of powers to a number of regional assemblies throughout the UK, by a Government which was persuaded that a less centralised structure would improve the governance throughout the UK, with Scotland accorded the same powers – no more, no less – as other regions, there would be no reason for either resentment or fears of instability to arise. In such a context there is no reason to expect that the business performance of the Scottish financial sector would be adversely affected.

Conclusion

Since for much of their business Scotland's financial institutions are dependent on the continued economic integration of the UK, full independence for Scotland would inflict serious damage on the Scottish financial sector. Many institutions would experience severe disruption to their business; the exigencies of marketing in the rest of the UK when Scotland was a foreign country would compel institutions to shift important functions to England; and the whole sector would suffer from the loss of these activities.

Though the economic integrity of the UK need not be compromised by devolution, the Scottish financial sector would suffer nonetheless either if devolution was seen as a prelude to full independence or if the process of setting up a devolved system of government for Scotland gave rise to resentment in the rest of the UK. It follows that a prerequisite for devolution to take place without damage to the financial sector is that it should not be a substitute for independence, but should instead be introduced in the context of a rational reform of the system of government in the UK.

Economic Independence and Political Independence

David King

Introduction

The principal purposes of this paper are to explore two of the key economic issues that arise in the context of possible Scottish independence. One of these issues is how the Scottish economy is currently performing and the other is how far an independent Scotland, assuming it remained within the EU, could pursue independent economic policies with the aim of improving its economic performance. The arrangement of the paper is as follows. The second section gives a brief background note, the third section compares the current state of the Scottish economy with those of other EU countries, and the fourth and fifth sections consider the scope for independent economic policies.

There are, of course, other economic issues which arise in connection with independence. One of the most debated issues has been the question of a Scottish budget or Scotland's fiscal balance. Given the widespread discussion of this issue (for an early treatment, see King 1973), there seems little point in covering the ground again here. In fact, using currently available data, it is impossible to get an accurate budget for Scotland or any other part of the UK. In general, given that Scotland generally enjoys a relatively high level of government expenditure per head and given that its output per head is rather below the average, it would be expected that it would have a somewhat less favourable – or more unfavourable – budget position than the UK as a whole. But such conclusion overlooks the complex issue of the allocation and tax proceeds of North Sea oil.

Whilst the truth about the balance is not known, its size is probably sufficiently small that the truth would sway few people one way or the other. If it was proved that the balance is adverse and that there is a net subsidy to Scotland from the rest of the UK, then it is unlikely that many people who favour independence would be persuaded instead to seek to preserve the Union: for anyone who supported an independent Scotland would doubtless feel that the loss of any likely level of subsidy from the rest of the UK was a price worth paying. If, in contrast, it was proved that the balance was favourable and that Scotland actually subsidized the rest of the UK, then it is unlikely that many people who are now Unionists would decide instead to support separation: for they would doubtless feel that any likely level of subsidy was a price worth paying for the benefits of continued union.

A Background Note

In view of the contentious nature of the issues discussed here, I should declare at the start that I am English. So, despite having lived in Scotland for 16 years, I might be assumed by some Scottish readers to be prejudiced in favour of retaining the Union. Conversely, of course, some English readers might assume that, as I have deserted their country, I probably favour severing any remaining links with it at Westminster.

In fact, my main interest in economics has always been with multi-level government, and in this context one of my main concerns lies in determining what level of government – or what size of jurisdiction – is most appropriate for various economic functions. From an economic perspective, there would clearly be a strong case for some form of Scottish government if it seemed that some government functions could be handled most appropriately by a body that covered an area and population roughly the size of Scotland. It is the aim of later sections to consider how far there is, in fact, an economic case for such a body.

Of course, the debate about independence transcends economic issues. But the interesting and important non-economic arguments for and against independence, and the balance between them, are outwith the scope of this paper.

The Scottish Economy

In discussing the economic prospects of a separate Scotland, it seems important to begin by saying something about the Scottish economy. In particular, it seems useful to make some comparisons between Scotland and the UK as a whole, and also to make some comparisons between Scotland and the rest of the EU. Tables 1, 3, 5 and 6 give data for intra-UK comparisons while Tables 2, 4 and 7 give data on EU comparisons.

Perhaps the key economic statistic for any country is its income per head since this is a useful indicator of its citizens' living standards. The two most usual measures of income are gross domestic product (GDP), which measures income generated by production in the country, and gross national product (GNP), which adds in net flows of profits, interest and other property income from abroad. For the UK, and probably Scotland, the two are almost identical.

In Table 1, column *(1)* gives 1991 figures for GDP per head for all the UK regions and also for the UK as a whole. The table ignores the output of the continental shelf which is not officially part of any region. Column *(1)* shows that Scotland's output per head was £8,234 which was about 3.3% below the figure of £8,516 for the UK as a whole. But in fact Scotland's figure is higher than those of any other region save the South East, East Anglia and the East

TABLE 1   GROSS DOMESTIC PRODUCT PER HEAD, [1] DISPOSABLE INCOME PER HEAD,
THE AVERAGE PROPENSITY TO SAVE AND CONSUMERS' EXPENDITURE PER HEAD: UK
REGIONS: 1991

Region	GDP per head[1] (£) (1)	Disposable income per head (£) (2)	Average propensity to save (3)	Consumers' expenditure per head (£) (4)
North	7,587	6,454	0.15	5,468
Yorks & Humberside	7,803	6,481	0.14	5,580
East Midlands	8,358	6,776	0.12	5,948
East Anglia	8,550	6,928	0.08	6,395
South East	9,925	8,043	0.08	7,419
South West	8,024	6,693	0.02	6,552
West Midlands	7,835	6,489	0.09	5,904
North West	7,891	6,742	0.09	6,112
Northern Ireland	6,567	6,112	0.12	5,349
Wales	7,365	6,059	0.05	5,755
Scotland	8,234	7,103	0.18	5,821
UK	8,516	7,071	0.10	6,381

[1] Excluding continental shelf.
Source: *Regional Trends 28* 1993 Edition, 132 and 137.

Midlands; and Scotland would need to be credited with only a quarter of the
UK's continental shelf production to be second only to the South East.

How typical was 1991? This question is answered in Table 2. There, columns
(1) and *(2)* show GDP per head in Scotland and the UK as a whole for each
year from 1981 to 1991. Column *(3)* shows the Scottish figure as a percentage
of the UK one. It is interesting to note that Scotland's relative position was
exactly the same in 1981. In between, Scotland's figure initially improved
vis-a-vis the UK, reaching 97.6% in 1983, and then fell back, down to 92.7%
in 1989. These variations are relatively modest, and it is noteworthy that even
in 1989 Scotland's GDP per head was exceeded in only three other regions.
The reason for the variations seems to be that Scotland is relatively resilient
to recessions and so compares most favourably in the most recessed years. Its
resilience to recessions may stem from the fact that the high interest rates in
recession years dampen consumer spending most in the South East where
house prices and mortgages are highest.[1]

Further evidence of Scotland's relative prosperity comes from column *(2)*
of Table 1 which shows that personal disposable income per head – that is
income after allowing for taxes and transfers – is just about the UK average
in Scotland. Indeed Scotland's figure is higher than that of any other UK
region save the South East. Scotland's relative position has varied a little over
the years. In Table 2, columns *(4)* and *(5)* show personal disposable income
per head in Scotland and the UK as a whole for each year from 1981 to 1991.
Column *(6)* shows the Scottish figure as a percentage of the UK one. Comparing column *(6)* with column *(3)*, it can be seen that variations in Scotland's
relative personal disposable income per head tend to move in line with the

TABLE 2   GDP PER HEAD AND PERSONAL DISPOSABLE INCOME PER HEAD:
SCOTLAND AND THE UK: 1981–1991.

	GDP per head			Disposable income per head		
	Scotland	UK	Scotland:UK	Scotland	UK	Scotland:UK
	(£)	(£)	(%)	(£)	(£)	(%)
Year	(1)	(2)	(3)	(4)	(5)	(6)
1981	3,542	3,663	96.7	3,004	3,120	96.3
1982	3,883	3,983	97.5	3,290	3,386	97.2
1983	4,252	4,358	97.6	3,622	3,664	98.9
1984	4,440	4,610	96.3	3,866	3,924	98.5
1985	4,890	5,112	95.7	4,181	4,235	98.7
1986	5,336	5,632	94.7	4,473	4,644	96.3
1987	5,786	6,167	93.8	4,832	5,043	95.8
1988	6,411	6,907	92.8	5,209	5,606	92.9
1989	7,036	7,590	92.7	5,667	6,186	91.6
1990	7,747	8,227	94.2	6,389	6,656	96.0
1991	8,234	8,516	96.7	7,103	7,071	100.5

Sources: Regional Trends 20 1985 Edition, 120, *Regional Trends 21* 1986 Edition, 120,
Regional Trends 22 1987 Edition, 128, *Regional Trends 27* 1992 Edition, 133 and
137, and *Regional Trends 28* 1993 Edition, 132 and 137. Note that the 1989 and
1990 comparisons of personal disposable income per head are a little unsatisfactory
as the community charge was introduced to Scotland in 1989 and to England and
Wales in 1990.

variations in its relative GDP per head. It can also be seen that Scotland usually
fares a little better in terms of personal disposable income than in terms of
GDP.

In Table 3, column (1) gives figures for GNP per head for all EU countries.
No figure for Scotland's GNP per head is published, but it can be estimated
as between $15,817 to $18,090 depending on what fraction of continental shelf
production was considered to belong to Scotland.[2] Comparing these figures
with the EU average of $18,058, it can be seen that Scotland would have an
income a little below or close to the EU average. It may be added that the EU
is, of course, one of the most prosperous regions in the world, and the range
of figures for Scotland would place it about 15th in the list of 127 nations
covered by the World Bank's statistics (World Bank 1993: 238-9).

Whilst Scotland enjoys a GNP per head as high as many EU countries, its
population and hence its total GNP are necessarily quite small. Its population
is 5.2 million and, if its GNP per head were at the bottom of the range noted
above, its total GNP would be around $80 billion. These figures can be
compared with the population and GNP figures of other EU countries shown
in columns (2) and (3) of Table 3, though this table excludes Luxembourg
whose population and GNP are each less than a tenth of Scotland's. Aside
from Luxembourg, Scotland's population exceeds Ireland's and equals
Denmark's, while its GNP exceeds those of Greece, Ireland and Portugal. So
if Scotland became a separate member of the EU from the rest of the UK,
resulting in the EU having 13 countries instead of 12, then Scotland would be
tenth equal in population terms and ninth in GNP terms.

TABLE 3   GNP PER HEAD, POPULATION, GNP, GNP GROWTH AND INVESTMENT
SHARES: EU: 1991.

Country	GNP per head 1991 ($) (1)	Population mid- 1991 (millions) (2)	GNP 1991 ($ billions) (3)	Average growth of GNP per head 1980–91 (%) (4)	Investment as share of GNP 1991 (%) (5)
Belgium	18,950	10.0	189.50	2.0	20
Denmark	23,700	5.2	123.24	2.2	17
France	20,380	57.0	1,161.66	1.8	21
W Germany	23,650	62.1	1,468.67	2.2	21
Greece	6,340	10.3	65.30	1.1	17
Ireland	11,120	3.5	38.92	3.3	19
Italy	18,520	57.8	1,070.46	2.2	20
Netherlands	18,780	15.1	283.58	1.6	21
Portugal	5,930	9.9	58.71	3.1	n.a.
Spain	12,450	39.0	485.55	2.8	25
UK	16,550	57.6	953.28	2.6	16
EU[1]	18,058	326.5	5,895.87	1.9	20[1]

[1]EU figures exclude Luxembourg and, in column *(5)*, Portugal also.
Sources: Columns *(1)*, *(2)*, *(4)* and *(5)* from World Bank *World Development Report
1993* (Oxford: Oxford University Press) 239 and 255. Column *(3)* from columns
(1) and *(2)*.

A source of strength for Scotland comes in the growth of income. As noted
earlier, Scotland's GDP has kept pace with that of the UK as a whole over the
period 1981-91; and column *(4)* of Table 3 shows that in the period 1980-91,
the UK had a growth rate higher than all EU countries save Ireland, Portugal
and Spain. The only caveat to this healthy growth is that column *(5)* of Table
3 shows that in 1991, at least, investment in the UK was a relatively low share
of GNP. The Scottish picture here is not much healthier: Scotland's 1990
investment per head in agriculture, energy, manufacturing, transport and
dwellings was comparable with the UK average (*Regional Trends* 1993: 139).
However, there is some consolation in the fact that the ratio of saving to
disposable income in Scotland, as shown in column *(3)* of Table 1, is higher
than in any other UK region. It is this high saving in Scotland which puts
consumers' expenditure per head there, shown in column *(4)*, in sixth position
for the regions despite disposable income being in second place.

Comparable incomes per head do not necessarily create comparable living
standards. One problem encountered in some countries is rapid population
growth which requires large expenditures to be devoted to new social capital
and infrastructure. This is no problem in Scotland where, in contrast, there
has been concern at a falling population. A major worry with such a fall is the
fear that it reflects an emigration of young skilled workers. Table 4 explores
the population changes of the UK regions between 1981 and 1991. Columns
(1) and *(7)* show respectively the 1981 and 1991 populations. Columns *(2)*
and *(4)* show the changes from natural causes and migration in numerical
terms while columns *(3)* and *(5)* show them in percentage terms. Column *(6)*

TABLE 4   POPULATION AND POPULATION CHANGES: UK REGIONS: 1981–91.

Region	Population 1981 (1)	Natural change 1981–91 (2)	Natural change as % of 1981 (3)	Migration 1981–91 (4)	Migration 1981–91 as % of 1981 (5)	Total change as % of 1981 (6)	Population 1991 (7)
North	3,117	18	0.58	−51	−1.64	−1.06	3,084
Yorks & Humberside	4,918	65	1.32	−29	−0.59	0.73	4,954
East Midlands	3,853	76	1.97	97	2.52	4.49	4,026
East Anglia	1,895	29	1.53	167	8.81	10.34	2,091
South East	17,011	452	2.66	96	0.56	3.22	17,558
South West	4,381	−6	−0.14	348	7.94	7.80	4,723
West Midlands	5,187	138	2.66	−70	−1.35	1.31	5,255
North West	6,459	88	1.36	−169	−2.62	−1.26	6,377
Northern Ireland	1,538	115	7.48	−59	−3.84	3.64	1,594
Wales	2,814	25	0.89	48	1.71	2.60	2,886
Scotland	5,180	27	0.52	−107	−2.07	−1.55	5,100
UK	56,352	1,027	1.82	270	0.48	2.30	57,649

Source: Regional Trends 28 1993 Edition, 44.

shows the total change in percentage terms. Column *(6)* shows that the total change for Scotland was a fall of 1.55%, the highest drop for any region. Column *(5)* shows that Scotland suffered from net emigration of 2.07%, though this figure was exceeded in both Northern Ireland and the North West. However, column *(3)* shows that Scotland's natural change was the lowest of any region at 0.52%. If Scotland's natural change had equalled the national average of 1.82%, Scotland's population would have fallen by only a third of the recorded fall.

Aside from population changes, economic problems can occur with a sparse population since there may then need to be high spending per head on roads and transport. In 1991, Scotland had a population density of only 64.8 people per square kilometre (*Regional Trends* 1993: 30). Column *(1)* of Table 5 gives comparable figures for all EU countries and it can be seen that only Ireland has a lower figure. However, the figures for Greece and Spain are only a little higher, and even France has a density only about 50% higher than Scotland's. While sparsity may be against Scotland's interest, its low dependency ratio – that is a low ratio of people outside the labour force to people inside it – can perhaps be seen as an advantage. Its ratio is the same as the UK's, at 1.0% (*Regional Trends* 1993: 30); column *(2)* of Table 5 shows that only Denmark enjoys a lower figure.

TABLE 5   POPULATION DENSITIES, DEPENDENCY RATIOS, EMPLOYMENT AND
UNEMPLOYMENT: EU: 1990

| Country | Persons per sq. km. | Dependency ratio | Employment (%) | | | Unemployment rate (%) |
| | | | Agriculture | Industry | Services | |
	(1)	*(2)*	*(3)*	*(4)*	*(5)*	*(6)*
Belgium	146.0	1.2	2.7	30.5	66.8	7.3
Denmark	119.3	0.8	5.7	27.6	66.7	8.0
France	104.3	1.3	6.0	30.0	63.9	8.7
Germany	252.0	1.0	4.2	40.3	55.5	4.9
Greece	77.4	1.5	22.2	25.7	52.1	7.0
Ireland	50.8	1.6	14.0	29.0	57.0	14.2
Italy	191.4	1.4	8.5	32.2	59.3	9.8
Luxembourg	147.3	1.4	3.5	28.9	67.6	1.6
Netherlands	364.6	1.1	4.4	25.6	70.1	7.4
Portugal	107.3	1.1	17.4	34.0	48.6	4.2
Spain	77.2	1.6	10.9	33.0	56.1	16.4
UK	235.2	1.0	2.3	31.2	66.5	6.9
EU	156.1	1.3	8.5	30.7	60.9	8.3

Source: *Regional Trends 28* 1993 Edition, 30–31.

Earlier tables looked at the level of output and incomes. The pattern of output is also of some interest. Some insights into this are provided by the employment figures in columns *(3)*, *(4)* and *(5)* of Table 5. These show that, on average, agriculture, industry and services account for respectively 8.5%, 30.7% and 60.9% of EU employees. The figures for Scotland are 3.1%, 30.4% and 66.5% (*Regional Trends* 1993: 31). Thus Scotland has a very low percentage in agriculture – only Belgium at 2.7% and the rest of the UK at around 2.2% have lower figures. And Scotland has a relatively high percentage in services – only Luxembourg at 67.6% and the Netherlands at 70.1% have higher figures. A low agricultural sector and a high services sector can be considered signs of a mature, highly developed economy.

Further insights into the pattern of output in Scotland are shown by Table 6 which compares the output figures of the main industrial groups for Scotland with the UK as a whole. It must be stressed that these figures relate to output rather than employment and are thus not directly comparable with the figures noted in the last paragraph. Columns *(1)* and *(3)* of Table 6 show the output of the main industrial groups in Scotland and the UK while columns *(2)* and *(4)* show the percentages of output contributed by each group. Comparing columns *(2)* and *(4)*, the main conclusion must be that the pattern of output is really very similar in Scotland and the UK as a whole. On the negative side for Scotland, the main differences occur with the ownership of dwellings and with financial and business services: for the services provided by owner-occupied dwellings and by the financial and business service industry each account for a share about two-thirds of their share in the UK as a whole. On the positive side, Scotland has rather more important agriculture, forestry and fishing, energy and water, and education and health industries.

TABLE 6   OUTPUT BY INDUSTRY GROUPS: SCOTLAND AND THE UK: 1990

Industry	Output in Scotland (£m) (1)	Share of output in Scotland (%) (2)	Output in UK (£m) (3)	Share of output in UK (%) (4)
Mineral, metals and chemicals	1,347	3.41	19,719	4.17
Metal goods, engineering and vehicles	3,589	9.08	45,112	9.55
Other manufacturing	3,709	9.38	40,977	8.68
Agriculture, forestry and fishing	1,162	2.94	8,753	1.85
Energy and water supply	2,110	5.34	18,662	3.95
Construction	3,140	7.94	35,616	7.54
Distribution, hotels, catering and repairs	5,757	14.56	71,865	15.21
Transport and communication	2,847	7.20	33,487	7.09
Financial and business services	3,650	9.23	60,992	12.91
Ownership of dwellings	1,522	3.85	30,254	6.41
Public administration and defence	3,012	7.62	31,647	6.70
Education and health services	5,043	12.76	44,815	9.49
Other services	2,641	6.68	30,431	6.44
Total	39,528	100.00	472,330	100.00

Source: *Regional Trends 28* 1993 Edition, 135.

Aside from output and growth, the economic variables of most concern are unemployment, inflation and the balance of payments. For many years Scotland suffered relatively high unemployment compared with the UK as a whole, but this position has recently changed. Columns *(1)* and *(2)* of Table 7 show the figures for Scotland and the UK for the period 1966-92 while column *(3)* shows Scotland's figures as a percentage of the UK's figures. The Scottish figure was higher than the UK one in every year until 1992, when Scotland's better figure reflected its relative resilience to recessions that was noted above. But the Scotland figure was, on average, 55% above the UK one in the first half of the period covered by the table and only 22% higher in the second half.

It is, admittedly, rather disingenuous to paint a rosy picture in a period when unemployment rose so much, and it is fair to add that Scotland's unemployment rate was, on average, 1.54% above the national average in the first half of the period, and 1.86% above it in the second half. But while the recent figures around 8-10% are clearly serious, Scotland can at least take some consolation from the fact that the 1990 level of 8.2% was just below the EU average which is shown as 8.3% in column *(6)* of Table 5. This column also shows that two countries – Ireland and Spain – had unemployment rates about double the Scottish rate.

TABLE 7   UNEMPLOYMENT RATES: SCOTLAND AND THE UK: 1965–1991

Year	Scotland (1)	United Kingdom (2)	Scotland: UK (3)	Year	Scotland (1)	United Kingdom (2)	Scotland: UK (3)
1966	2.7	1.5	180	1980	6.8	4.8	142
1968	3.7	2.4	154	1982	11.3	9.5	119
1970	4.1	2.6	158	1984	12.5	10.7	117
1972	6.3	2.9	217	1986	13.3	11.2	119
1974	3.0	2.0	150	1988	11.3	8.2	138
1976	5.0	4.1	122	1990	8.2	5.8	141
1978	5.9	4.4	134	1992	9.5	9.7	98

Sources: *Economic Trends Annual Supplement 1993*, 133–4; *Regional Trends 28* 1993 Edition, 94.

With inflation, no separate Scottish figures are published, but the Scottish position is likely to be very similar to that in the UK as a whole. Column *(1)* of Table 8 shows that the average UK rate in the period 1985-93 was 5.08%, a little above the EU average of 4.16%. But the UK rate has been falling lately so that, as shown in column *(2)*, in 1991-92 it was 3.76%, somewhat lower than the EU average of 4.26%; and, as shown in column *(3)*, by 1992-93 it had fallen to 1.50%, little over half the EU average of 2.90%

With the balance of payments, Scotland's situation could be radically different from that of the UK as a whole. Unfortunately, the position is really impossible to gauge as there are no reliable figures for trade between Scotland and the rest of the UK. Perhaps all that needs to be said is that the UK as a whole has a sizeable current account deficit on the balance of payments and it is unlikely that Scotland on its own has a very much better situation, though it is to add the caveat that any continental shelf production allocated to an independent Scotland would help considerably.

The UK's 1991 position is shown in columns *(4)*, *(5)* and *(6)* of Table 8 which concern visibles, invisibles and the overall current balance for all EU countries. In 1991, the UK's current deficit equalled 1.17% of GNP which was a little over the EU average of 1.00%. The UK current deficit widened a little in 1992 and early 1993. Some help has since been given by the depreciation of sterling which followed its withdrawal from the EU exchange rate mechanism (ERM) in September 1992.

To sum up, this section has shown that anyone who is tempted to regard Scotland as a depressed region of the UK is quite wide of the mark. Despite suffering from major declining industries for much of the century, Scotland is now one of the most productive and prosperous regions of the UK with a high income per head and, currently, a below average unemployment rate. Growth has recently been relatively high compared with the EU though the percentage of output accounted for by investment is currently a little lower than the EU average. The rate of inflation is very low. The balance of payments situation is unclear: there could be a substantial deficit on current account though this might be reduced or even reversed if a newly independent Scotland was able to secure title to a large fraction of continental shelf production.

TABLE 8   INFLATION RATES, AND VISIBLE, INVISIBLE AND CURRENT BALANCES AS PERCENTAGES OF GDP: EU.

Country	Average inflation 1985–93 (%)	Inflation rate 1991–92 (%)	Inflation rate 1992–93 (%)	Visible balance 1991	Invisible balance 1991 (% of GNP)	Current balance 1991
	(1)	(2)	(3)	(4)	(5)	(6)
Belgium	2.29	2.36	2.22	−0.36	2.69	2.33
Denmark	3.10	2.10	0.79	3.96	−2.14	1.83
W Germany	2.24	3.97	3.74	1.57	−2.93	−1.35
Greece	16.97	15.87	13.73	−15.40	13.38	−2.03
Spain	5.97	5.86	3.58	−6.21	2.92	−3.29
France	2.87	2.33	1.95	−0.86	0.30	−0.56
Ireland	2.97	3.13	1.04	8.28	−3.44	4.84
Italy	5.42	5.21	3.39	−0.07	−1.91	−1.98
Luxembourg	2.25	3.11	3.11	–	–	–
Netherlands	1.72	3.78	1.87	4.20	−0.99	3.21
Portugal	10.20	9.08	5.22	−13.40	12.30	−1.10
UK	5.08	3.76	1.50	−1.91	0.74	−1.17
EU	4.16	4.26	2.90	−0.58	−0.41	−1.00

Sources: Columns *(1)*, *(2)* and *(3)* derived from price index figures in Office des Publications Officielles des Communautés Européennes *Eurostatistik: 6 1993* (Luxembourg) 106. Columns *(4)*, *(5)* and *(6)* derived from trade figures in *Eurostatistik: 6 1993*, 121–2 and GNP figures in Table 3.

Independent Economic Policies – An Overview

Before discussing the scope for independent Scottish economic policies, it is helpful to recall the main types of economic policy. Following Musgrave's (1959: 5) classification, these policies are generally placed under the three headings of stabilisation, redistribution and resource allocation. There are two strands of thought in the economics literature which help to shed some light on how much freedom a Scottish government might be able to have over these three areas of policy.

The first strand is that concerning small countries (see for example Leddin and Walsh 1990). This shows that the scope for independence in stabilisation at least, is typically very modest for small countries. This issue is discussed in the next but one section, following a brief account of the difficulties with stabilisation faced by all countries.

The second strand is the branch of economics known as fiscal federalism. This considers, *inter alia*, how the three main areas of economic policy might be divided between central and local government within a country. It has tended to conclude that while local authorities might have an important role to play in terms of resource allocation, central governments should have the principal roles of stabilisation and redistribution (see for example King 1984: 6-49). This might seem an irrelevant issue to the question of Scotland's possible independence, because it would seem that Scotland's central government would have no less scope for independent stabilisation and redistribution policies than a UK government. However, there are developments in the EU which threaten to make independent stabilisation policies – and even perhaps independent redistribution policies – more difficult for any Member State. Effectively these developments are progressively making the EU the central government for its area, and thus the fiscal federalism literature seems to have equally important lessons for both a putative Scottish government and the UK government.

Stabilisation Policies – Problems Faced In All Countries

The standard macroeconomic model presented in economics textbooks suggests that the economy settles at an equilibrium level of output and at an equilibrium level of prices that are each determined by the overall level of demand – that is aggregate demand – and the overall level of supply – that is aggregate supply. The main concern is whether the equilibrium level of output is the one which secures full employment, or rather which secures a rate of unemployment described as the 'natural rate' of unemployment. The natural rate allows that there will always be a tendency for some unemployment. There are various reasons for this. For instance, the flow of school and college leavers entering the market may not exactly match the flow of retiring people who are leaving it; also, there will always be some people who resign their present jobs before seeking others; and there are always some people who have been made redundant because their skills are no longer required, and these people may have to spend some time retraining before they can secure new jobs.

On this model, governments are seen as trying to adjust aggregate demand and hence output until unemployment is at the natural rate. It is important that unemployment does not fall below the natural rate, for if it does, then there is likely to be inflation, possibly at an increasing rate. If the current level of demand does result in unemployment being below the natural rate, then employment and inflationary pressures can be reduced by reducing demand. Conversely, if the current level of demand results in an output level that leaves the rate of unemployment above the natural level, then employment can be increased by raising demand. A clever government would use monetary or fiscal policies to adjust – or fine-tune – demand until the equilibrium level of output was just sufficient to secure unemployment at the natural rate. In this way, there would be no unemployment other than natural unemployment, and there would also be no inflationary pressure, unless there were pressures by unions for higher wages, by firms for higher profits, or increases in import costs.

Such a model gives a deceptively simple view of how a government could seek to remove unemployment without creating inflationary pressures. If things really were that simple, it is hard to see why any country would be enduring much unemployment or much inflation, let alone both which has been a common situation in the 1970s and 1980s.

Some of the difficulties with stabilising economies apply to countries of any size. One problem is that it is not easy to know what the natural rate of unemployment is. Another problem is that aggregate demand is typically rather unstable, especially its investment component, so that maintaining full-employment equilibrium would in principle need constant fine-tuning by the government. This might be feasible were it not for the problem of lags. By the time the government has recognised the need for action and taken action, and by the time the action has had any effect, the situation might have changed of its own accord so that quite different action might be appropriate.

Another problem with stabilisation is that all economies are open and trade with each other. Suppose a government has indeed achieved an equilibrium output level where the only unemployment is natural and there is no inflationary pressure. The government might find that the country had a balance of payments deficit on current account with exports and property income paid abroad falling short of imports and property income received from abroad. To finance the deficit, the country would have to borrow from abroad. This would mean keeping interest rates at a level needed to attract foreign capital. But once interest rates were constrained in this way, monetary policy could no longer be used to fine-tune demand. And higher interest rates might dampen investment and so reduce growth. An alternative strategy would be to allow the country's currency to depreciate and so make home products more competitive with foreign ones, but this would raise the price of imports and so threaten to spark off inflation.

This brief account shows that operating successful macroeconomic policies is difficult. Almost invariably, policies designed to improve one aspect of the economy create difficulties elsewhere. Indeed, some economists adopt the view that governments should not attempt macroeconomic stabilisation. In simple terms, these economists argue that governments should keep the money stock rising in line with rises in output, in the hope of maintaining stable prices, and that they should eschew other stabilisation policies. If, at times, demand is too high or too low to secure unemployment at the natural rate, then eventually wage rates will adjust so that the labour market will end up with unemployment once again at the natural rate. Any attempt by the government to fine-tune demand with monetary or fiscal policies is, because of lags and uncertainty, as likely to do harm as good.

On this approach, there would be no scope for a Scottish government, or indeed a UK or EU level of parliament, to have a successful independent stabilisation policy. But even if this rather extreme view is rejected, it must be accepted that operating stabilisation policies is hard. And there are special problems in small countries which must now be examined.

Stabilisation Policies – Problems Faced by Small Countries

One of the problems faced by small countries is that they typically have especially open economies and this makes it hard for them to have much effect in their areas. One measure of openness is the level of imports as a percentage of GNP. Imports in the UK as a whole account for around 27% of GNP. For any smaller area, such as Scotland, the percentage will be much higher. In Ireland, for instance, imports account for around 65% of GNP, and in Belgium, where land links with neighbouring countries reduce transport costs, the figure is 80%. In such circumstances, efforts by central governments to raise output and employment by using fiscal policies could have very limited impact. For instance, cutting taxes might result more in a large rise in imports – creating employment elsewhere – than in a rise in local production. And a rise in government spending, perhaps on higher public sector wages, could have similar consequences. A more effective strategy might be to raise public expenditure on construction, but even here there could be a substantial import component in the construction materials, and the tendency for large fractions of any extra construction workers' wages to be spent on imports means there would be very little in the way of induced second-round multiplier effects (discussed in King 1981).

It may be added that fiscal policy will be even weaker than indicated above if the government of the small country concerned adopts a managed float or freely fluctuating exchange rate regime. For if fiscal policy does succeed in raising aggregate demand and incomes, then it will also create a rise in interest rates because the rise in incomes will raise the demand for money. The rise in interest rates will increase capital flows from abroad, creating a balance of payments surplus and hence a rise in the foreign exchange value of the country's currency. This rise will tend to choke off exports and raise the demand for imports as opposed to import substitutes, thereby reducing aggregate demand.

Leddin and Walsh (1990: 78) have cited the openness of the Irish economy as the major reason why 'there is widespread agreement that...fiscal policy is not an effective instrument' there. And Walsh (1987: 19) has estimated that if the Irish government's surplus or deficit was changed by a substantial 1% of GNP, unemployment would change by only 0.4%. Thus there might be a change in unemployment from, say, 10.0% to 9.6%. Moreover, much of this fall might disappear in the long-run. One reason why some of the fall would be temporary is that sooner or later the government would have to raise taxes to help start repaying the extra borrowing.

The high import propensities of small economies also create problems with monetary policies. For any attempt to raise demand by reducing interest rates could lead chiefly to a large rise in imports of capital goods and consumer goods. There is a further problem that it might in fact prove difficult to reduce interest rates in the first place. If capital is mobile between countries, as it is within the EU and also between the EU and many other countries, then any country which seeks to have lower interest rates than those prevailing elsewhere is likely to see a flight of capital from itself to other countries. This means that it will experience a severe balance of payments deficit. If the country operates a fixed exchange rate regime, then it will have to reverse its expansionary monetary policy and raise interest rates again to restore balance of payments equilibrium. If the country operates a flexible exchange rate regime, then it will find its currency depreciating so that exports rise and imports fall and the demand for import substitutes rises. The effects of rising output will include a rise in incomes and hence a rise in the demand for money, so there will be a tendency for interest rates to rise back towards their original levels.

In fact, with capital mobility, interest rates tend to equalise in all countries. The only caveat to this conclusion is that interest rates will be above world levels in countries whose currencies are expected to depreciate and *vice versa*. This makes it hard for small countries to operate independent monetary policies. Of course big countries, such as Germany and the United States, have a little more discretion as they play a leading role in determining what the world level of interest rates is to be. It is clear from recent events within the EU that members have found very little freedom to set interest rates independently of those operating in Germany. Admittedly the UK was able to reduce interest rates *vis-a-vis* Germany after Black (or White) Wednesday in September 1992, but this was chiefly because the UK devalued that day so that UK interest rates no longer needed the premium that applies to countries whose currencies are thought likely to depreciate.

It might be wondered if an independent Scotland could try to circumvent these constraints on its monetary policies by restricting capital mobility with various controls. There are two reasons for supposing that it could not. One is that these controls are no longer permitted within the EU. The other is that Scotland has a strong financial sector whose future would be critically put at risk by any hint of capital controls.

This analysis points to the limitations of monetary and fiscal policy in small economies. But it has also indicated an apparently hopeful alternative, namely exchange rate policy. For it has been suggested that if a small country operates a flexible exchange rate regime and undertakes an expansionary monetary policy, then the resulting fall in interest rates will create a depreciation in the value of its currency. This will raise output and, whilst the rise in output raises incomes and the demand for money, and so in turn raises interest rates to offset the original fall in interest rates, that original fall had nevertheless created a rise in output and a fall in unemployment. Certainly economic analysis suggests that this seems the most feasible policy for an independent Scotland.

However, there would be problems with an active fluctuating exchange rate policy. One problem, of course, is that this policy option might not be available for very long because moves towards monetary union within the EU mean that the EU would try to restrain countries from operating such policies. Another problem is that Scottish exporters might find that exchange rate uncertainty added to the risks of their investment decisions, so they might cut back on investment in Scotland; indeed they might prefer to expand elsewhere in the EU. Given that, as a small economy, Scotland would have a large export sector, this is an especially important point. Certainly none of the small EU countries at present favours a policy of fluctuating exchange rates.

A further problem with a fluctuating exchange rate is that a depreciation might have only a temporary effect. If Scotland's currency fell in value, then clearly Scotland's products would initially be cheaper for foreigners while foreign products would initially be more expensive for Scots. So there should be an increased demand for Scottish products. However, the cost of Scottish products could soon rise. One reason is that the cost of imported raw materials would rise. Another reason is that as Scots found imports rising in price, and home produced products with an imported raw material component rising in price, so they might seek wage increases to compensate. Wage rises would raise the cost of Scottish products so that demand for exports would fall and demand for imports would rise. Ultimately, the only effect of the depreciation might be that Scotland's currency would have fallen x% while Scottish prices had risen x%, so there would be no lasting effect on output and employment at all. This scenario is particularly important for small economies where a rise in the home price of imports will be significant. In an analysis for Ireland, Flynn (1986) estimated that a 10% fall in the exchange rate would be wholly offset by a rise in Irish prices within two years. Given the long history of many common prices and wages between Scotland and the rest of the UK, it is possible that the offset would operate much more quickly in Scotland.

Independent Economic Policies – The Fiscal Federalism Approach

At the heart of fiscal federalism lies an appreciation that preferences may vary in different parts of a country. Thus there is a *prima facie* case for decentralising to subcentral levels of government any decision where decentralised decision-making is feasible. These subcentral levels of government might be states or local authorities in a federal country but only local authorities in a unitary country. Such decentralisation enables different preferences to be catered for. One of the key issues in fiscal federalism lies in identifying those aspects of government policy where decentralisation is feasible. The conventional wisdom, perhaps first espoused by Musgrave (1959: 179-82), is that it is not very feasible to decentralise redistribution or stabilisation, though it might be feasible to decentralise many aspects of resource allocation.

The main problem with decentralising redistribution is that any subcentral authority which sought to have higher taxes for the rich than other areas in order to finance more generous transfers to the poor would run the risk of driving its rich citizens away and attracting more poor citizens in. Consequently its policy could prove unsustainable. Indeed, on this analysis, it can be seen that all subcentral authorities would be liable to find themselves obliged to pursue policies comparable to those in the area whose citizens desired the least amount of redistribution, so it would be the voters in that least redistributive area who would determine the degree of redistribution throughout the country. Such problems should generally be less serious with central governments since, typically migration is much harder between countries than it is within countries.

However, it is clear that migration between EU countries is much easier than it used to be, and so it seems equally clear that individual EU countries have less room for manoeuvre with redistribution policies than they used to have. Indeed their hands are now tied not only by the easing of regulations concerning migration within the EU but also by EU policies on redistribution. These policies can be justified in part on the grounds that they are necessary to prevent each EU country from having to adopt the policies of whichever EU country has the least amount of redistribution. The most notable declaration on this issue was contained in the Social Chapter of the Maastricht Treaty which was adopted by all EU members except the UK. The Social Chapter is principally about workers' rights and much of it concerns items such as the length of the working week and holiday entitlements which touch only peripherally on redistribution. But the Chapter also obliges the signatories to move towards common policies – though admittedly not common absolute amounts – on minimum wages, and it obliges them to work towards common goals for their systems of welfare payments. So if Scotland seceded from the UK and joined the EU as a signatory to the Social Chapter, it would find limited room for freedom. And it must be debatable whether the EU would admit Scotland as a new member if it did not sign up to the Social Chapter.

Of course limited freedom is not the same as no freedom, and the existence of language and cultural differences within the EU means that there are barriers to migration which ensure some scope for independent distribution policies. But even aside from the Social Chapter and the rest of the EU, Scotland would face the further constraint that there have long been close ties and substantial population movements between it and the rest of the UK. Any attempt by Scotland to have significantly higher tax rates or more generous transfers than elsewhere in the UK could promote emigration of the rich from Scotland and immigration of the poor into Scotland. Thus an independent Scotland could still find itself closely tied to the policies adopted in the rest of the UK.

The problem with decentralised stabilisation is rather different. It is essentially the difficulty of finding any suitable instruments for a subcentral authority to use. It would not be able to use exchange rate policies or tariffs and quotas because each subcentral authority would use the same currency and because tariffs and quotas are always prohibited within countries. It could not use monetary policy because all subcentral authorities use the same currency whose amount is the responsibility of the central bank. The only remaining tool is fiscal policy. Certainly it would be feasible for subcentral authorities to contemplate deficit financing if they wish to raise aggregate demand, although their high import propensities would mean that their policies might have little impact on output in their own areas. But there are two related reasons for supposing that the access by subcentral authorities to deficit and surplus financing should be strictly limited.

First, if there were no limits on deficit financing, some authorities might seek to use debt finance simply in the expectation that by borrowing to finance their current spending they could shift the tax burden of that spending away from current citizens and taxpayers on to the future citizens who would be obliged to pay the taxes needed to repay the loans. Second, a subcentral authority's debt could make its future residents as a whole worse off. To the extent that the debt is held by local residents, the taxes needed to repay it will merely redistribute income from future local taxpayers to future local debt holders. But to the extent that the debt is external, there will be a redistribution from future local taxpayers to future non-resident debt holders. As most local authority debt is external, it requires future local residents to pay higher taxes and to transfer income to citizens elsewhere.

Although an independent Scotland would be an independent country, not a subcentral authority, these issues would still be relevant. It would still seem unsatisfactory for an independent Scotland to seek to raise aggregate demand by using deficit financing since that would transfer the burden of paying for local services from current Scottish taxpayers to future Scottish taxpayers. Also, as a member of the EU, where capital can now flow freely between countries, there could well be a substantial non-resident holding of any Scottish debt. So Scottish borrowing today could require a transfer of income from future Scottish taxpayers to people living outside Scotland.[3] So a Scottish government might well feel it should make only very limited use of deficit finance.

Quite aside from its own feelings over borrowing, an independent Scottish government would probably be constrained in its use of debt finance by the EU. For if Scotland were to accept the Maastricht treaty – and it is doubtful if Scotland would be allowed to enter the EU otherwise – it would be constrained by the rules there for public sector borrowing. These stipulate that public sector borrowing should not exceed 4% of GNP and that public sector debt should not exceed 60% of GNP. Admittedly the chief aim of these rules is reduce the temptation for members to finance public deficits with new money, thereby having rapid monetary growth and aggravating inflation, so making monetary union more difficult. But if members were to meet these and other goals and secure monetary union, then it is doubtful if rules on public sector deficits would be significantly eased.[4]

Conclusions on Independent Economic Policies

This paper points to a rather negative view on the prospects of an independent Scotland operating a wide range of independent economic policies, especially if it were part of an EU where monetary union were to proceed. It is legitimate to ask, then, how Ireland, which must suffer from similar constraints, has managed to have a significantly higher rate of growth than the UK since around 1960; for instance, column (4) of Table 3 shows that between 1980 and 1991 the Irish economy grew on average at 3.3% per year while the UK economy grew on average at only 2.6% per year. This question on Ireland's higher rate of growth was put to the present Irish Taoiseach, Albert Reynolds, in 1991 when he was Finance Minister. He cited three factors that had helped Ireland (Reynolds 1992). One was the country's increasing openness to external trade, especially with its entry to the EU, along with its active involvement in the 'building of economic and monetary union within the EU'. Another was its package of measures – which include a 10% rate of corporation tax on manufacturing firms – to stimulate international investment. And the third was its successful attempts to secure EU funding of infrastructure improvements.

One conclusion from this answer is that Ireland would not recommend an independent Scotland to refrain from EU membership. But such membership implies numerous constraints on economic policy, as mentioned earlier, and

TABLE 9   SEATS AND VOTES IN THE 1992 GENERAL ELECTION: SCOTLAND AND THE UK

Party	No. of seats (1)	UK: % of seats (2)	% of votes (3)	No. of seats (4)	Scotland: % of seats (5)	% of votes (6)
Conservative	336	51.6	41.9	11	15.3	25.7
Labour	270	41.5	34.4	49	68.1	39.0
Liberal	21	3.2	17.9			
Democrat				9	12.5	13.1
Nationalist	7	1.1	2.3	3	4.2	21.5
Other	17	2.6	3.5	0	0.0	0.8

Source: *The Herald* 11 April 1992, 1.

it can be seen that only the second of the factors noted by Reynolds really seems to count as an independent economic policy. Could an independent Scotland perhaps hope to imitate this policy and attract more international investment than it does now? It is doubtful if it could. The main problem is that the EU is anxious to move towards a common policy of taxing company profits. The low Irish tax rate on manufacturing firms may not have resulted in much pressure for harmonisation because Ireland is small and there is an awareness that its GDP per head is well below the EU average. But the pressure for harmonisation could well be substantial if an independent Scotland sought to imitate this policy. Such pressure might be instigated by Scotland's southern neighbour which would probably stand to lose most of what Scotland gained.

In contrast to independent stabilisation policies, Scotland could undoubtedly have significantly different resource allocation policies on matters such as education, health and transport. These are the sorts of issues that are often cited as being appropriate for a devolved Scottish assembly. The argument for such an assembly, and for equivalent regional assemblies elsewhere in the UK, is that at present policies are imposed by a Conservative government which, as columns *(1)*, *(2)* and *(3)* of Table 9 show, has a majority of seats at Westminster despite having less than 42% of the votes cast in the 1992 election. There are some areas of the country where other parties obtained a majority of the votes. With regional assemblies, different policies could operate in different areas to reflect differing preferences.

This is an attractive view and there is much to be said for devolution as a concept. Indeed, there is much to be said for devolving power as much as possible, whether it is to individuals, small local authorities, regions or nations within the EU. But while there may be a strong case for devolving some resource allocation functions that are now handled at Westminster, a careful study would need to be made to see if those functions could not be given to smaller areas rather than large regions such as Scotland. For opinions vary within Scotland as well as between Scotland and the rest of the UK. This variety within Scotland can be seen clearly from column *(6)* of Table 9, which shows that there the four major parties each secured over one-eighth of the Scottish votes in 1992, even though columns *(4)* and *(5)* show that Labour secured an overwhelming majority of Scottish seats. It may be that a Scotland-wide assembly would prove best for some functions such as health and main roads, but it would be rather imprudent to assume this and establish a devolved Scottish assembly without seeing whether it was true. Certainly it is arguable that most of the functions proposed for devolution in the 1979 referendum might more appropriately have been handled by three large local authorities which would cover Scotland between them (see King 1980).

In conclusion, the question noted in the second section may be restated. Are there any functions for which a government the size of Scotland seems most appropriate? In the case of stabilisation, it has to be said that EU central governments are between them looking more and more like lower levels of government with limited powers of action. The recent (1993) virtual break-down of the ERM is certainly a blow for those who seek monetary union, but it is clear that there is a substantial wish for such union in the EU, and even the UK government, with its proposals for a hard ECU, seems to accept that the *status quo* is not a long-run equilibrium. If and when monetary union occurs and there is a European central bank, member countries will lose all powers over monetary and exchange rate policy, and they are likely to find their fiscal policy powers, such as the power to run surpluses or deficits or to operate favourable tax rates for industry, heavily circumscribed. It might be an exaggeration to say that the existing EU central governments will have no independent stabilisation powers, but their stabilisation powers would be so small that it is hard to enthuse about the prospect of a Scottish government getting hold of them.

If the Scots really want an independent stabilisation policy, they would be better to secede from both the UK and the EU. It is clear that this situation would not be advocated for Ireland by Reynolds, and it is not the current policy of the SNP. But it is worth noting that the most prosperous European countries in terms of a high GDP per head are actually Switzerland, Sweden, Norway and Finland. It must be noted, though, that Sweden, Norway and Finland are seeking EU membership and in 1994 they took a preliminary step towards full EU membership by combining with the EU to form the new European Economic Area. And even outside the EU, Scotland's history of links with the rest of the UK could still impose various constraints on the extent to which Scotland could adopt independent policies.

In terms of redistribution, it must be wondered if Scotland could feasibly be much more progressive than the rest of the UK. There would probably be scope for only modest differences, and this scope is likely to be constrained by the EU in future. Resource allocation, then, offers much more scope for independent policies. But there remains the question of whether any resource allocation function that could be taken over by a Scottish assembly might not be better entrusted to smaller authorities so that policies could vary within Scotland as well as between Scotland and the rest of the UK.

In short, there might be some prospects for independent economic policies for an independent Scotland outwith the EU, although secession from the EU would also carry risks of economic isolation. But it is difficult to see much scope for an independent Scotland within the EU pursuing policies very different from those in the rest of the UK and the rest of the EU. Incidentally, the arguments suggesting that an independent Scotland within the EU might have limited autonomy also apply in considerable measure to all the existing EU countries. The debate on what, if anything, their central governments should do in the post monetary union years is surely one to which attention must soon be given.

The Foreign Dimension: Choices for Scots

John Thomson

The Scots are, beyond doubt, a nation, but Scotland is not at present a State. The issue is whether Scots should now seek to make Scotland an independent sovereign state de-linked from the UK or whether, on balance, they would prefer to remain within the UK. Possible constitutional developments within a UK including Scotland are another matter.

Donne's aphorism, 'No man is an island, entire of itself; every man is a piece of the continent, a part of the main; ... ' is pertinent to the issue. 'No man is an island' applies nowadays to nations as well as to individuals, even to nations who inhabit an island. The idea that nations have a divine right of independence is as much a myth as 'the purity of the race'. Neither dogma has ever been true: they are the doctrines of fanatics and people of insular mentalities. They are particularly untrue in an age of over-population, easy communication and global markets. The notion that multi-national states are outdated (Scott 1992: 27) is a sad fallacy which, if taken seriously, would lead to chaos and rapine. There are more than 2,000 nations.[1] If even only one quarter of them sought to follow the example set in parts of Africa, in ex-Yugoslavia and in the former Soviet Union, there would be an end not only to the United Nations (present membership: 184) but also to international law and order.

Multi-national and multi-cultural states have existed since long before the Roman Empire and they seem set to be the pattern of the future. If it were not so, it would mean the dominance of absolutism and the physical oppression of minorities. These are evils against which the civilized world struggles. The penalty for failure could be a future dominated by the clash of 'civilizations' as the latest scholarly fashion has it (Huntington 1993: 22-49). Far more likely is it that the dominant themes will be the ebb and flow of power between the rich and the poor within states and within civilizations and the introduction of revised concepts of justice which will help to justify the difficult but inevitable readjustments of the balance of power worldwide. Short of nuclear war, it is improbable that any state[2] or even nation will seek an island status (in Donne's sense) wrapped in her 'purity' and self-righteousness.

In considering the choices in front of Scots, we can, therefore, safely dismiss a future as 'Ultima Thule,' a tartan paradise unconcerned (except, perhaps, in football) with the real world of commerce and art, of influence, exchange rates and jobs. It would not be worth scorning such a notion if it were not that it has been hinted at or at least implied in some self-indulgent ruminations. When it comes to choices for their future, Scots need to be hard-headed.

Speaking practically, the Scots have three broad options. They are the Danish option, the Norwegian option and the UK option. The first represents a Scotland which has broken away from the UK and taken her place in the world community as a sovereign state and an independent member of the European Union (EU).[3] The second is the same but without membership of the EU, while the third leaves the Scots within the UK, within the EU, and without an independent state though not necessarily without some modification to the existing constitutional arrangements.

The choice among the three options cannot sensibly be based solely on how they look at this narrow moment: we also have to consider the probable future. Donne's aphorism recalls the importance of 'the continent.' We need to make a judgment about the developments underway in the EU and also about the longer term prospect for the character of the EU and for the balance of influence within it. The future of the EU is, in turn, closely linked to global trends and so we will need to glance at these. Donne also bade us look to 'the main.' Divorce from England would be a traumatic event for many, and the process would do much to shape the character of a Scottish state at least in its early years. We need to consider this and the process of negotiation which it would begin, on the one side, with England as sovereign state to sovereign state and, on the other side, with the EU and its constituent states for the establishment of Scotland's place as a full member of the EU. In passing, we should pause for a moment to note the controversy about the legal issues involved in Scotland's application for membership of the EU, but this is not the place in which to resolve them definitively. Even after all this, we are still not quite adequately prepared to make a choice, for it would be unrealistic to leave out of account some of the arguments of emotion that resonate in the public debate. For example, 'better a small voice than no voice at all' (Scott 1992: 44). Whatever the intrinsic merits of such slogans, they arise from a yearning for an emotional satisfaction that is largely absent at present. In politics, emotions can matter as much as pounds and pence.

Such is the framework of this essay. By choice, the issue is viewed in the perspective of the foreign dimension, which is not to deny the relevance of other dimensions. A conclusion will be reached, but there will be no pretence that it can be all-embracing or definitive throughout the eons. Whatever decision is made now, circumstances change. Whatever choice the Scots make, they will not cease to be a nation capable of making new choices.

The Danish Option

The similarities between Scotland and Denmark are striking. Both are northern European countries with a Protestant ethic and a well educated population of just over five million. Both have respected traditions of seafaring, fishing and multifarious activities beyond the sea which have sustained their national spirit, especially vis-a-vis their large neighbours to the south. Both populations have strong instincts towards what might be termed anti-authoritarianism, and both are determined to maintain their nationhood. Each is affluent and has a high standard of living. It is therefore reasonable to suppose that what the Danes can do the Scots can do likewise.

Danish relations with Germany are satisfactory and Denmark's standing in the EU is good: she is a respected, cooperative and useful member of the EU. Until her two referenda in 1992 and 1993, Denmark had seemed like most of the smaller states in the EU to favour an ever closer union leading ultimately perhaps to a federal state of Europe. The referenda showed that the Danes were less willing to entrust their future to the bureaucracy in Brussels and more nationalistic than had been supposed. In this they have shown themselves to be closer to Scottish ways of thinking than had been assumed. In short, on the face of it, there seems no reason why, after the initial problems of independence have been surmounted, Scotland should not occupy a place in the EU similar to Denmark's. The vision of St. Andrew's cross flying alongside fifteen or more European flags at the Breydel Building is attractive; but it is not self-evident that it would be to the advantage of the majority of Scots. This needs hard-headed examination.

On the plus side, Scotland would become a member in good standing of what may be (depending upon the progress of the North American Free Trade Agreement) the world's largest trading bloc. This would ensure that Scotland would have some, though limited, influence in the formation of the EU's trading policies. It would mean that Scotland would enjoy free trade (or something approaching it) within the EU and would be protected in the squalls of international trade negotiations by the ample umbrella of the EU. It is true that for the sake of EU solidarity Scotland, like other members, would have to submit to certain compromises of her national interests, but she would have some limited room for manoeuvre in striking bargains.

If the EU prospered, Scotland could expect to prosper with it, though whether this was to the same extent as other members, e.g., Denmark or England, would greatly depend upon hard work and the skill with which the Scottish economy was managed. Yet the management of the Scottish economy could not be wholly autonomous. Like other members, Scotland would be affected by interest rates determined elsewhere in the EU, by the pattern of subsidies, by regulations governing agriculture, industry, communications, environmental matters, etc. Scotland would have some voice, though not much of one, in the terms on which the membership of the EU was further expanded. The same would be true of negotiations for the deepening of the EU towards an 'ever closer union.' In any event, she should assume that in the long run she would surrender more sovereignty to Brussels.

The terms on which Scotland joined the EU would be for negotiation and would be important. For none of the other two or three dozen international institutions which Scotland would wish to join is it likely that serious negotiations would be required. There is no need to mention them all. It is axiomatic that Scotland would become a member of the United Nations and of its many agencies, including the IMF and the World Bank. Given Scotland's traditions, it is unthinkable that Scotland would not become a member of NATO and would not be welcomed as such. Presumably, she would also wish to join Western European Union (WEU).

All these advantages now enjoyed by Denmark (with the exception of WEU) would be enjoyed by Scotland. However, in essence they are the very same advantages which Scots already enjoy within the UK. Whether Scots if they became like Danes would enjoy them to the same extent as at present or more or less would significantly depend upon two conditions, which are touched upon later in this essay. The first is the weight at which Scotland would punch in international institutions and especially in the EU. The second is the quality of Scottish leadership and the skill of Scottish negotiators.

The minus side of the Danish option is that Denmark is a small, not a large member of the EU and of other international institutions, and moreover that any advantages gained in negotiations will have their reciprocal costs. What Scotland would have to pay cannot be precisely determined until the date and circumstances of independence are known. Nevertheless, the Danish figures probably provide the best guide available.

The following are key indicators taken from the latest statistics available.[4] Denmark's annual 'subscriptions' to the EU, to NATO and to the UN (excluding the agencies) are respectively £884.4m, £10.09m, and £3.849m. The annual cost of Danish diplomacy, i.e., Diplomatic Service plus international aid is £839m. The Danish defence budget currently stands at £1.783m.[5]

If one adopts the simple expedient of dividing the current UK figures by eleven, roughly in proportion to the population of Scotland, an approximate comparison can be made with the Danish expenditure. On that basis, Scotland is contributing to the 'subscription' to the EU, to NATO and to the UN (excluding the agencies) £222m, £15.69m, and £3.1m per annum. Her contributions to the diplomatic and defence budgets on the same basis are £4.92m and £2.147m.

One or two comments are called for. For an independent Scotland, the initial costs, i.e., over the first 5-10 years, would be significantly greater than stated above. Scotland would have to re-provide a lot of infrastructure for both diplomacy and defence. If UK assets were divided proportionately to population (a fairly favourable assumption for Scotland, the 'demandeur') Scotland would get one in eleven of British embassies and other missions abroad and a similar percentage of defence installations. Scotland probably already has one-eleventh of the latter and maybe more, but they are not, of course, designed to form a coherent whole. Moreover, the Danish figure for defence expenditure would probably not sustain the existing Scottish regiments, let alone a navy and an air force. So the establishment and maintenance of Scottish defence services would on present form be an expensive business. The same is true of diplomacy. The initial costs would include not only the purchase or renting of real estate round the world, but also the cost of creating a new diplomatic bureaucracy and of providing it with sophisticated communications equipment, etc. Denmark gives a lot more aid per capita than the UK does, but even if an independent Scotland were to stick to UK aid levels, one eleventh of the UK diplomatic budget would barely suffice to maintain relations in Europe, let alone with such important trading partners as the US, Canada, Australia and Japan.

These are not insuperable problems, but they do underline the inescapable fact that Scotland is, in European terms, a relatively small country and, if independent, would suffer from the opposite of economies of scale. Given the fierceness of international competition, she certainly could not afford to reduce expenditure on infrastructure, research, investment or education. Indeed, almost certainly, Scotland would need to increase expenditure under each of these headings.

Though it is difficult to establish exactly comparable figures, it is worth noting that whereas Scotland's expenditure on education is £3.296m, Denmark's is £6.098m. On the one-eleventh basis, Scotland's contributions to the UK costs of social security is £5.893m whereas Denmark spends £21.295m under the same heading. Despite these significant disparities, there would not be the same need in education and social services as in diplomacy and defence to re-provide infrastructure with consequent sharp increases in expenditure in the initial years of independence.

The crucial point for expenditure is that since Denmark manages, there is no fundamental reason why Scotland should not do likewise. There would, of course, be a cost. Danish income tax is 50% at the basic rate and 68% at the top rate. Currently, UK figures are 20% for the standard rate and 40% at the top. The rates for an independent Scotland would almost certainly have to increase considerably over the current UK figures, especially initially, but could settle down to something similar to the Danish figures for costs in relation to benefits.

The Norwegian Option

If Scotland is like Denmark, she is also similar to Norway. The latter, it is true, has a much larger land mass and a smaller population (4.262m) but these are disadvantages compared to Scotland's situation. On the other hand, Norway probably has access to larger oil and gas reserves.[6] Taken all in all, Norway provides a reasonable indication of what Scotland's situation would be were Scots to opt for a sovereign state separate from the UK but, unlike Denmark, not a member of the EU.

The Norwegians have so far consistently though narrowly rejected the possibility of joining the EU, despite the invitation held out to them for the past twenty years or so. They have been influenced by the same sort of considerations as moved the Danes to reject the Maastricht Treaty in their first referendum. They value their independence and their Nordic-ness; they fear these could be submerged in a large community of which they would form only a small part; they distrust the Brussels bureaucracy; they do not want to be committed to major decisions on money, federalism and nationality until the final moment for choice arrives; they are apprehensive about the effect of the free movement of people within the EU boundaries, and so on. In addition, they are wary about the future of their fishing industry and about the risk to their North Sea oil and gas resources. If Scots broke away from the UK, many might share Norwegian attitudes.

Despite the serious doubts of a large part of the electorate, the current

Norwegian government favours membership of the EU, and together with three other members of EFTA – Sweden, Finland and Austria – has successfully negotiated to join the EU, probably in 1995, subject to the result of a referendum to be held in late November 1994. The outcome at present is too close to call. This, in itself, is a matter on which Scots will want to ponder. A society deeply divided on a fundamental issue such as whether to join the EU or not may become unhappy and could squander much of its creative energy in the dispute. It would be damaging to the Scottish spirit if a bruising debate on whether or not to break away from the UK was immediately succeeded or accompanied by a close fought controversy on whether or not to join the EU.

The advantages of joining the EU as set out under the Danish option are attractive and, furthermore, there would be no significant savings in not doing so. It must be admitted, however, that Norway, with the cushion of her oil and gas revenues, has hitherto managed more than adequately outside the EU. Nor has she felt isolated. As part of the Nordic Group, Norwegians have colleagues and a cultural home. Separated from the rest of the UK and from what was the Empire, Scotland lacks this. However, it is perhaps not beyond the bounds of possibility that an independent Scotland could be considered for membership of the Nordic Group and especially so if Norway remained outside the EU.

On the other hand, if Norway herself goes over to the Danish model, Scotland would be almost totally isolated in Europe. This would be uncomfortable even if the economic disadvantages of non-membership of the EU turned out to be surprisingly mild. This alone would almost certainly influence Scots against the Norwegian option. If the Norwegian referendum leads to Norway joining the EU, only the Danish model will remain as a serious option at this time. But if Norway continues outside the EU, it may be worth looking closely at her budget and taxation policies. The costs to the diplomatic and defence budgets of re-providing facilities would presumably be the same as with the Danish option, but the uncertainties would be greater. If it is hazardous to compare Danish figures with one-eleventh of UK figures, it is still more so to compare each of them with current Norwegian costs, subsidies and taxes. Yet it could and must be done if the Norwegian option is really to be considered seriously.

Whatever the result of the Norwegian referendum, it would seem disadvantageous for Scotland to be outside the EU with England in it. It would be excessively odd, not to say awkward, if EU regulations led to England discriminating against Scots in favour of Irish, French, Greeks, etc. From this position, to have to make a special arrangement with England perhaps rather on the lines of the arrangement East Germany formerly made with West Germany, would be humiliating as well. If England is in the EU, Scotland, in her own self-interest, has to be likewise. The Irish faced exactly this situation when the UK joined the EEC and unhesitatingly decided to join too, which as events have proved, was much to their advantage.

If still another argument for being within the EU is required, the issue of inward investment supplies it. The UK has received more investment from the US and Japan than any other country in the EU. There have been various reasons for this, but undoubtedly a prime one is the knowledge that UK-made products have free access to all EU countries. If an independent Scotland could not hold out this inducement to investors and England could, the latter would have an enormous advantage in attracting foreign money. The effect on the financial services located in Edinburgh and on industry throughout Scotland would be grim. And this would come on top of the loss of EU agricultural and regional subsidies.

The case against the Norwegian option is conclusive on all grounds except perhaps those of sentiment and emotional satisfaction. The arguments applying to the Norwegian option reveal how closely Scottish interests are tied to trade with England and also how much the two countries would be in competition for inward investment. The Danish and Norwegian options both suffer from the probability of relatively high capital costs in the first years of independence. Such costs, though hobbling in the short term, could probably be managed and especially so if the longer term future seemed rosy. The degree of difficulty which a newly independent Scotland with her own new currency would encounter depends crucially upon the terms of the divorce from England. That is not the sort of dependency for which one would wish as the basis for a proud, independent state. We return below to the divorce proceedings, but meanwhile we should look at the arguments for and against the UK option.

The UK Option

The advantages, disadvantages, costs and opportunities of this course are familiar. For this reason, they risk being taken for granted and in practice partly overlooked. The generality of Scots have only a cloudy notion of what is bad and what is good for them in the UK. As yet, few people in England have ever thought about Scotland's position in the Union.

This situation is itself a large part of the reason for the current discontent. Scots feel that the English take them for granted. As a distinctive nation they want their voice to be heard, but it is sometimes hard to discern that the English are listening. This is partly because Scots speak with several voices, as do the English. But when the voice of Scotland is heard unambiguously as in the last four General Elections, Scots find themselves under a government which they actively do not want. So, for some time, the normal processes of democracy have tended to exacerbate the political feelings of Scots and have made many feel they would rather have democracy within Scotland than democracy within the Union.

There is a good deal to this attitude, for it is more that than a rational argument. Apart from the possibly exceptional situation arising from four unsatisfactory General Election results in a row, there is always a doubt whether Scots' voices and Scottish interests are clearly heard and ardently supported when international negotiations take place and the decisions are made. The majority of Scots probably do not think there is any large degree of ill-will involved. Whitehall plays fair by its own standards, and statistically

Scotland does rather well within the UK. Yet there persists a feeling which cannot be ignored that somehow the distinctively Scottish voice gets drowned out by the remaining ten-elevenths of the UK and that a separate Scots voice in Brussels could be in the interests of the Scots people.

The reality is, as usual, more complicated and more interesting than the stereotype. Not only are there several Scottish voices, but there are various, not wholly compatible Scottish interests. The way in which the Scottish and English voices are blended is not constant. And then there is the Scottish Office. Does it accurately hear Scottish voices and perceive Scottish interests? If it is hard for the authentic voices of Scots to get through to decision-makers, the Scottish Office provides the first sieve. The second and the third are provided by the bureaucracies in London and in Brussels. A chief attraction of the Norwegian option is that it eliminates the second and third sieves. Similarly, a prime attraction of the Danish option is that it eliminates the London sieve. The presumption is that the voices of the Scots will be heard more clearly and more influentially if there is only one sieve or perforce two.

With Brussels in full swing is London necessary? Indeed, is it not a drag upon Scottish energies and Scottish initiative? The answer is: sometimes yes, sometimes no. But then if one asks about the Scottish Office, one gets the same answer. If one goes on, 'the Scottish Office is inevitable' even if it ought to be subject to more intense public scrutiny, it is hard to avoid, given what has been argued above, saying the same about the Brussels bureaucracy. With the rise of Brussels, London is perhaps not so inevitable but the question then is whether the advantages of London or the UK outweigh the disadvantages.

If the advantages of the UK option were not taken so much for granted, they would be dazzling. In the short term, the UK option means that Scotland avoids a messy divorce and the relatively high capital costs of the early years of independence. Both in the short and in the long term, Scots enjoy through the UK option the advantages of EU membership and of a respected and relatively stable currency. For the foreseeable future, the larger EU governments will wield significantly more influence than the smaller ones. The UK has an access and an authority which except in special circumstances, Denmark lacks. Scotland's voice, heard through the UK, is amplified in Brussels and worldwide. Yet, it must be admitted, it is not a purely Scottish voice: it is a UK voice.

One way of stating the issue is: do the Scots want to speak with a purely Scottish voice? Put this way, the thought is seductive and invites the answer 'yes.' That in turn almost certainly means independence and very probably the Danish option. But this is not the only way of stating the issue. Another and more sophisticated way is to accept that the Scots care about many things besides nationalism and to ask a group of questions which respond to these cares. Through which option will Scots achieve the best standard of living? What will be the best framework to take care of hard times such as global recession, adverse technological change leading to loss of competitive edge, environmental disaster, external threat whether through terrorism, mass migration, nuclear proliferation or a trade war? Under which option will Scots most influence the world? How will they best promote their concerns for freedom, democracy, the rule of law, justice for minorities, human rights, the protection and lifting up of the poor, the advancement of the disadvantaged, the feeding of the hungry, the humbling of the oppressors? How will Scots most effectively give expression to their strong streak of kindliness?

The answer, on balance, to all these questions is through the UK option. To choose the Danish option is not to claim these are irrelevant questions or to choose a path that cannot produce answers to them. But there is little doubt that the UK can furnish the Scots with better and more complete answers. The UK has more clout internationally than does Denmark. That is a fact of which Scots have been keenly aware for a long time. If you were picking countries for a global game of influence, you would choose the US before the UK, but you would choose the latter before Denmark.

The foregoing questions represent a series of values and ideals for which the UK (and Denmark too) stands. The traditions of British-ness have had a powerful influence round the world for some 300 years. The revolution of 1688 which established a degree of toleration and parliamentary government based on law was a Scottish as well as an English achievement. It was an event more significant for the world and indeed for the component parts of the UK than the union of 1707. The traditions to which Scots contributed so much both within these islands and beyond the seas have informed the constitution of the United States and the purposes and principles of the UN Charter. These values, adapting to modern circumstances, march on but they need invigorating and nurturing worldwide. Of course, Scots can pursue them under the Danish option, but they can pursue them more effectively under the Union Jack.

Patriotism is a virtue, but it is as much a virtue if it is exercised for the sake of the Union as for an independent Scotland. Shakespeare is part of British culture and so is Burns. Great Britain is more than a GB bumper sticker. In short, Britain is a reality, not an artificial construct. The Scots can remain a nation of 5.1 million and yet help to run a State with worldwide influence and be proud of it.

All that has been said so far about the three options arises from present circumstances. It will be prudent also to look ahead and see how the way the world goes may affect Scotland and the Union.

The Way of the World

If it was difficult to predict the abrupt vanishing of the Cold War with scarcely a whimper, it is yet harder to foresee the turbulent future. We have been taken unawares in uncharted waters and are not sure what stars to steer by. Different societies are tending to set different courses. These are not favourable circumstances in which to launch a new state, especially if that should provoke more divisiveness within the West.

Speaking, for the sake of brevity, in general terms, states and nations are trending towards a modern form of isolationism. In its benign shape it might be called individualism, in its ugly form, selfishness.

We in the West[7] are disenchanted with foreigners who keep presenting us with new problems when we already have enough at home. If people in Haiti, Somalia, Bosnia, Tajikistan, etc., refuse to forget their histories and decline to change overnight into liberal democrats, we are puzzled and then disgusted. Most of us see no reason to pay in money, lives or other resources for the mistakes of developing countries. Nor do we want to subsidise our neighbours who we suspect of unfair trade practices. It is true that financial institutions thrive on 24-hour bourses and multinationals on global markets. Yet the ordinary voters are encouraged by certain politicians to see only the competitive face of trade and to fear for their jobs and standards of living.

Coping with Eastern Europe and the ex-Soviet Union is more of a strain than we had expected, and nuclear proliferation and irresponsibility remain a danger. The West's view of most developing countries is, if anything, still more jaundiced. The old enthusiasms for development and democracy have become a shadow of their former selves. They are still there, but not many voters are ready to sustain them with taxes, lost jobs or other sacrifices. Expectations have dwindled: politics looks like a cash dispenser in some Third World countries, and poverty like a genetic defect. Third World poverty is linked in Western minds with huge population increases, destruction of the environment, mass migration, threats to jobs and shameful neglect of human rights. Ethnic conflicts leading to oppression of minorities, contempt for liberal democracy and even to ethnic cleansing seem to be on the rise. In short, to many in the West much of the Third World looks like a bottomless pit and ungrateful, too.

Simultaneously, confidence in international institutions has declined. No wonder, for international institutions can only do what their members, the governments, want and are willing to pay for.

Despite this litany of woes, it is within the power of the West to cope with all of them provided this is done prudently, progressively (i.e., not all at once) and above all, unitedly. The overriding requirement is for the West to hold together and cooperate. If a common purpose and a readiness to compromise for the mutual good informs Western policies, there is no problem which cannot be surmounted. This will require confident leadership, e.g., in the G7.[8] The results of the Uruguay Round in GATT are mildly encouraging.

The evolution of the EU can play an important role in encouraging Western cooperation or the reverse. If Europe falls to squabbling, it will be bad for the Europeans in particular but also for the solidarity of the West. The official policy of the EU holds that it should be widened and deepened. It is probably impossible to do both simultaneously, but it is far from certain that we will get our priorities right. At any rate, this is not a conjuncture which is favourable to a third dimension of change, namely the splitting of existing members. 'Europe of the Regions' has its attractions as a Platonic notion, and in the form of a consultative organ representing regional authorities it is a practical possibility, but in the full sense of the term it could, in present circumstances, lead to a disintegrating Europe.

If, nevertheless, the debate between Scots is resolved in favour of the Danish option, two negotiations will ensue. The first will be the divorce from England

and the second, over-lapping it, a negotiation to settle Scotland's rights, privileges and obligations as an independent member of the EU.

The Divorce

The precise circumstances in which Scots decided to constitute themselves as an independent state and the sentiment of public opinion on both sides of the border at that time cannot be certainly known in advance. For present purposes, however, the following assumptions may be regarded as a reasonable approximation to reality:

—The English would acquiesce in Scottish independence but would not go out of their way to make it easy.

—The Scots would be 'demandeurs' and therefore would start with the weaker negotiating position and would be more vulnerable to procrastination.

—Each point in the negotiation would proportionately matter more to Scotland than to England, probably including the division of North Sea oil and gas revenues, a matter which could give rise to lengthy litigation with oil companies and others.

—Once Edinburgh had opted for independence, London would have a positive incentive to direct investment away from Scotland and to reduce expenditure there.

If it is difficult to foresee exactly how and when the negotiations might get under way, it is still more so to predict their outcome. What can be said with a high degree of probability is that they could be difficult and especially so on the Scottish side. Even technically, there would be problems since the present Scottish Office bureaucracy is inadequate for the purpose and would need to be expanded. More importantly, the balance of negotiation on substantive points will tend to favour a larger England content with the status quo. Altogether, it would take a great deal of skill for Scotland not to find herself over a barrel in the divorce proceedings and this without any notable or counter-productive display of English ill-will. Nevertheless, the separation can be achieved and can even be achieved skilfully, but not easily and not with any degree of comfort unless Scottish opinion is undivided and firm for independence.

The Negotiation with the EU

The debate about whether an independent Scotland has or has not, legally speaking, a right to be considered as a successor state to the UK and therefore automatically to acquire membership of the EU upon independence is in practice beside the point. The matter has been learnedly argued and the best opinion probably is that the Act of Parliament in Westminster which legally constituted the divorce would have to be accompanied by legal and political action within the EU, probably Treaty amendment, which 'necessarily includes the concurrence of the Community institutions and all Member States'

(Lane 1991). Only thereafter would Scotland (and England) become a member of the EU. Whether this view is universally accepted or not, the fact is that Scotland would have to negotiate to settle a considerable list of practical questions, and it is virtually certain that this would lead to Scotland taking her place at the Council table as one of a dozen or so smaller members of the EU.

Thus, the legal issue is not of prime importance. More significant is the fact that it would be hard to conclude the negotiations with Brussels and the capitals until the divorce from England is complete. This gives London a considerable lever, especially as members of the EU will not feel obliged to go out of their way to help Scotland. Scotland will no doubt get benefits, but she will also have to make concessions. It would be a mistake, therefore, to assume that Scots will get more net benefits from the EU than they do at present.

The Attitudes of Member States of the EU

However unjust it might seem to Scots, most people in Europe would look on independent Scotland as one of a group of potential new members. Scotland's change of status from the UK option to the Danish option would seem less of a gain for the EU than the adherence of Sweden, Finland, Austria and Norway. It seems likely that all four of these countries or at least the first three, will be members of the EU before an independent Scotland can be. Then there is the deserving but difficult case of Turkey. In the next rank, Poland, Hungary, the Czech republic and the Slovak republic are desperately anxious to be admitted, but they all need massive subsidies of one sort or another. Behind them loom the imponderables further East and South, who need even more proportionately in the way of subsidies.

In this mass of supplicants, Scotland might well be considered as a special case similar in many ways to Norway. The addition of another Western European member to an EU which was already 15 or 16 strong would create few ripples. But by the same token, Scotland would not be in a strong position for seeking special favours. An extra member usually slightly dilutes the influence of existing members and an independent Scotland would bring no more to the EU than Scotland as part of the UK already does. The existing states would not see why they should pay for Scotland's independence, and it is hard to imagine that they would make important sacrifices to accommodate Scotland.

The Irish would no doubt genuinely and openly welcome the independence of Scotland unless, of course, they had reason to suppose that one defection from the UK might lead to another and result in the independence of Northern Ireland. A similar idea might cross the minds of Walloons and Flemings, but by and large the smaller countries would be more concerned about whether an independent Scotland might reduce their share of the cake than they would be about political implications. The opposite would probably be true of the larger countries. There would be a good many French, Spaniards, Italians and even Germans who would be concerned about the example set for Brittany and Corsica, for the Catalans and the Basques, for Lombardy and even for

Bavaria. It is unlikely that these concerns would translate into downright opposition to Scotland, but they could add up to a certain sympathy with England even if mixed with a degree of *schadenfreude*, and they would in general mean that an independent Scotland would be tolerated rather than welcomed with enthusiasm.

'Better a Small Voice than No Voice at All'

This heartfelt cry (Scott 1992: 44) encapsulates a great deal of the emotion of the debate between Scots. The implication that as things stand Scots have no voice at all in the UK or in the world is so contrary to the evidence that it is not to be taken seriously. But the emotional nationalism in this slogan must be considered seriously and respected. Emotion has its own reasons and they deserve examination. Is it better for Scots to have a small independent voice or to be part of the larger, more influential voice of the UK? What will be the balance between the larger and the smaller states within the EU?

The natural tendency is for small states to enjoy most influence when their adherence is crucial to an original contract or to a major development of it. The Benelux countries at the time of the Treaty of Rome and again at the admission of the UK to the EEC are instances of this. In this perspective, the timing of Scotland's independent membership of the EU, coming as seems likely when the EU is expanding, is unlikely to favour her.

Statistically, an independent Scotland's voice would be small and in an expanding EU would be growing smaller. Whereas Denmark is at present one amongst seven smaller countries, by the time Scotland joined the EU she would be one amongst ten or eleven or even more smaller members. There would still be the same number of larger members, namely five, France, Germany, Italy, Spain and the UK. Although the unexpected can always happen, the reasonable assumption is that the influence of the larger and richer states will grow proportionately whereas that of each of the smaller and especially poorer states will decline. It is inherently unlikely that the smaller countries, several of which are on the geographical periphery and at different levels of economic development, would find it easy to combine against the big central states. The classic option for smaller countries in such circumstances is to press for an ever closer union in which European-ness dominates and independent Scottish-ness declines. But that may not be what Scots want.

It cannot be doubted that the UK has more influence over the actions and character of the EU than an independent Scotland could aspire to have. Accordingly, it is likely that Scots have more influence within the EU now than they would have as an independent state, especially as the disparities in influence among the five bigger members of the EU and the rest grow. Capital will tend to concentrate in the bigger central states and the periphery will depend more on subsidies and lower wages. At any rate, the larger contributors to the EU budget are likely to have a larger voice than the smaller ones. To choose independence now would be to opt, even within Europe, for a declining degree of influence.

If the global position is considered, the loss of influence would be greater. Denmark is a European power; the UK has a wider reach. Since 1945 the UK has consistently punched above its weight even though below its hopes. Despite being a middle-sized country with a relatively declining economy, the UK has had great and disproportionate influence. For example, taken overall, it has almost certainly had more influence than Japan, China or India. Whatever the changing balance between countries, it is likely that the UK (with or without Scotland) will continue to exercise a degree of influence globally which is not justified by pure statistics. It would be unprofitable and even humiliating for Scotland to be frequently dependent upon England for trade and for influence.

Some Scots want independence from the English more than anything. Others want the nation of Scots to express itself politically, distinctively and in a united way. Both groups favour the slogan about a small voice. But other Scots who do not suffer from an inferiority complex vis-a-vis the English and who aspire to an important degree of influence in the world are proud of the Union. At any rate, a lot of people are used to it. Would such people be disappointed to find, after independence, that their country's influence had dwindled? Whatever the answer, it would be important for the citizens of an independent Scotland to show maturity and refuse to repine when it became apparent, as it would, that English influence was considerably more significant than Scottish. This brings us back to emotion.

In the life of a nation, influence and standards of living, important though they are, may not always dominate. The Scots are a proud and successful nation. If the only way to continue being Scots was to create an independent state, there would be many supporters of the Union who would hesitate. Yet in the UK, that is not the position. Satisfaction can be obtained in many ways. Emotional nationalism can be an important element, and there is little doubt that for some Scots the creation of an independent state would produce satisfaction. For others, the destruction of the Union would cause distress. The whole issue tends to set Scots against each other: it is not a happy debate.

Conclusion

It would be ridiculous to assume that Scots could not make a go of the Danish or even the Norwegian option, so, to that extent, the nation has a genuine choice. But to settle on a divorce because life afterwards is possible or because it gratifies nationalistic sentiment, an emotion which is causing unnecessary misery in many parts of the world, smacks of wilfulness. It would be different, if great principles were at stake as in the American Declaration of Independence, or if economic and political circumstances required it as in the formation of the European Community, but the reverse is true. The principles of tolerance and of pluralistic democracy favour the Union as do considerations of influence and standards of living. Scots can best serve their own interests as well as making a valuable contribution to the well-being of Europe and the world by remaining British as well as Scottish.

A Historical Perspective on the Union

Roy H Campbell

There is often much confusion about what exactly is meant by the Union of Scotland and England. It may be the Union of Crowns in 1603 or the Union of Parliaments in 1707, but, when union is considered in a longer-term historical perspective, it is evident that, apart from these formal unions of crowns or of parliaments, England and Scotland were thrown together in various ways over a long period of time – at different speeds and with many reverses – through a convergence of geographical, religious, family, economic and other interests. In many ways the formal unions were merely the upshot of such underlying trends. It is, however, to the Union of Parliaments in 1707 that most attention is directed because it still provides the framework by which the country is governed and so changes to it are proposed as ways of leading to what is expected will be better, more efficient and more acceptable government.

When the parliamentary Union of 1707 is viewed over a longer period it would seem to have, at least superficially, a more solid foundation for its continued survival than many others. Even though it was concluded only after a good deal of haggling, some of which shows the unedifying nature of much diplomatic negotiation, it was entered into freely by two sovereign states. Many other comparable unions have come about through conquest and colonisation. Wales was conquered and Ireland also, for a time at any rate. Where unions came about in continental Europe, they were often much less stable. The nineteenth century witnessed several of different durations. Norway and Sweden were joined in a personal union from 1814 until 1905; Belgium and the Netherlands from 1815 to 1830. Many of those of the twentieth century have ended in recent separation, disastrously in several cases. Only the union of Denmark and Norway, which lasted for over 500 years until 1814 exceeds the 300 or 400 years of the unions of Scotland and England. Of course, as in any marriage, there have been periods of greater or lesser success and acceptability, but any union which lasts so long would seem to have strong forces working in its favour, giving rise to a presumption against change. Why the historian may ask, has there been such a long period of survival? Why, in spite of times of unquestioned acceptance and others of serious criticism, has there been no general outright rejection? Why do so many now assume the Union has outlived its usefulness? Answers to such questions offer insights into the hazards which may be encountered in devising alternative arrangements.

Any form of union, even none at all, was likely to give rise to dissension simply because Scotland and England were so different in size and resources and because Scotland was the remoter part of an island off the continent of Europe when Europe was the pivot of much trade and of all accepted culture. Dependence, economic and political, is likely to be the portion of a neighbour in such a peripheral position, and is hardly likely to lead the smaller partner to accept association easily. It is indeed more likely to engender resentment and conflict. Even generous treatment by the larger or wealthier neighbour does not remove the suspicion. It can give rise to resentment which encourages the smaller to assert its rights and to be an irritant wherever possible. A similar response, and resentment, can be identified from any peripheral region towards the centre even within one country. The provinces are always suspicious of the power and influence of the capital. Glasgow is of Edinburgh; Wick is of Inverness. And within the UK the north-east of England, which is so similar in many ways to the industrial belt of the west of Scotland, sees its neglect by London as great, and as in need of special attention as any part of Scotland.

The effects of this old geographical factor – the one island which threw the Scots and English together – were reinforced by common dynastic and religious influences, though any increasing convergence was not always welcomed. The marriage of James IV to Margaret Tudor in 1503 meant that, throughout part of the century that followed, the heir presumptive to the English throne was the Scottish monarch. The religious factor was more complex and had wider cultural implications. The Bible was available to the people only in English. Tyndale's New Testament was in Scotland about 1527 and the first Bible printed in Scotland in 1579 was the Geneva Bible with no concessions in vocabulary or spelling to its Scottish readership. Given the widespread use of the Bible, often the only reading material available to many, its availability in English was an important influence in the cultural assimilation of the two countries. The Scots read what they regarded as matters of life and death in the words of English-speaking reformers. In the same common spirit the Scots saw closer association with England in the sixteenth century as the way of advancing the reformed faith. John Knox remarked to William Cecil, Elizabeth's adviser, that perpetual concord between Scotland and England would be effected by 'the preaching of Jesus Christ crucified'.

It seemed to some contemporaries that many forces were bringing the two countries together, not simply in greater harmony but in unity. James VI thought so and his accession to the English throne might have been expected to encourage the move towards greater integration. However, the century of regal union was not one of increasing amity, partly because contentious policies acceptable to the stronger partner were imposed on a reluctant weaker one, especially in ecclesiastical affairs.

The disputes of the seventeenth century, especially over religious matters and later in economic affairs, when the religious quarrels had abated and were mostly removed in 1690, illustrate well why some came to think the closer union of 1707 more desirable, even essential. They also explain exceptions allowed for in that closer union. Had the shared protestantism flourished and led to religious uniformity, as the earliest reformers expected, a major influence which was to keep the two countries apart, and which was to prove a disintegrating factor in union far beyond ecclesiastical affairs, would have worked in the reverse direction. Though both nations rejected the authority of Rome and opted for protestantism, the form found acceptable on both sides of the border differed. Accommodation of differences was difficult. A covenanted relationship with God was a central concept in much Scottish theology and it was developed to give a special place and authority to the nature of the Scottish Reformation. The Scots were deemed to have taken the place of the Jews since they had the most truly reformed and purest church on earth. When the theological concept was combined with the political reality of a reformation backed by an aspiring nobility, religious beliefs flourished in a way which augured ill for any accommodation with those who thought differently, whether Laudian high churchmen or Cromwellian independents. A nation which saw itself as elected and ordained by God as an agent of his predestined will was hardly likely to tolerate direction from England. Equally, as before, England was as unlikely as ever to tolerate direction from the smaller nation. The detailed differences have their own interest but the important consequence in any consideration of the Union is that a potentially major integrating factor with widespread cultural implications was reversed. The reversal is easily portrayed as an example of the imposition of unacceptable ways on the Scots by more powerful monarchs or by as unpopular a protector, but the famous words of the future Lord Protector to the General Assembly in 1650 suggests that the fault might have been as often with the Scots as with their opponents: 'I beseech you, in the bowels of Christ, think it possible you may be mistaken'. Those who held firmly to the belief in an elect nation could not be mistaken. Concessions, acceptable to some never satisfied all, but most did accept the ecclesiastical settlement of 1690, which established presbyterianism in Scotland. A major difference in national identity was fixed. Each country went its own way ecclesiastically, peacefully but critically tolerating one another. In that respect greater integration had not been realised, and it was to remain a distinguishing and a potentially disintegrating feature in any union of the two nations.

By the time of the Union of 1707 the influence of the religious factor was declining, and a major flaw in some Scottish historiography is the suggestion that until then the country was so torn apart by disruptive religious controversy that there was little progress in most other walks of life – cultural, social or economic. There was, however, always another more constructive side to Scottish life. One striking positive initiative towards modernisation in those years were measures by parliament and council to improve the performance of the Scottish economy. Their efforts are instructive because they draw attention to some problems which have a modern ring about them and which show the hazards in the economic relations of Scotland and England when following independent policies. Comparable issues have come to occupy a central – some would suggest the most critical – aspect of any discussion of the Union today.

The effort to improve economic performance is seen in the mass of legislation passed after the Restoration, though it embodied few new principles, and which was reinforced in a further bout of measures in the 1680s. The adoption of independent economic policies encountered such difficulties that the Scots were forced to seek remedies which showed the potential conflict of interest in two closely-knit economies. Since Scotland was the less powerful, it could not easily ignore English policy. When the English passed their Navigation Acts in 1660, the Scots responded with their own in the following year. That this response was pointless was evident when the burghs asked the King, through the Council, to be declared free of the restraints of the English acts, certainly a better way for the Scots but unlikely to appeal to the English. A similar problem emerged in August 1661 when gold coin in England was revalued and, to prevent speculative movements of specie, a similar proclamation had to be issued in Scotland. The economic integration based on the old geographical proximity meant that the currencies were so closely linked that an independent economic policy was hardly open to Scotland.

A major conflict of interests was almost inevitable. It came in the 1690s, a decade when the adverse effects of any economic policy were heightened by subsistence crises. A key problem of the economic policies of these years was that the planned expansion of domestic production had to be accompanied by a colonial policy which would provide the markets on which the surplus on the balance of trade could be built. Colonial schemes stretch back into the seventeenth century and were boosted after 1693 when the privilege of forming societies or companies was extended from manufacturers to merchants engaged in foreign trade. The Company of Scotland trading to Africa and the Indies (the Darien Scheme) came in 1695. Its history is well-known. It was misconceived by any standard but its failure was blamed on royal indifference encouraged by English intransigence and gave rise to deep Scottish resentment. Far from leading many to perceive the impracticalities of an independent economic policy when Scottish economic life was so closely interwoven with that of England, the Scots responded by hankering after even greater independence of action. It is easy to understand the reaction as an upsurge of emotional nationalist sentiment, but on a more rational analysis it can also be seen as a failure to understand the nature of the relationship of two closely linked countries in an expanding competitive international economy. The problem in the regal union was that the power of the monarch was limited, in practice as well as in law, and becoming more so, to settle any dissension between the two countries when vital economic interests were at stake. Given the mercantilist objectives of the time, neither party would have dreamt of giving way to the other. England as the bigger and economically the more powerful and more securely established, especially in the colonial trade, was not ready to allow Scotland to reap any benefit from hard-won colonial territories. Try as they might, the Scots could not emulate the achievements of the English with any success; worse still for them, their national pride was injured when they were forced to recognise any realistic assessment of their position. In years to come, the Scots were to enjoy some competitive advantages, but they were few until well into the eighteenth century. Until then, if they were to gain entry to its profitable trade it had to be with England's connivance and, when that was not available, some agreement had to be reached to allow them to do so. That dilemma could not be dismissed or ignored. Many at the time and subsequently have misinterpreted events by assuming that the English should have been ready to accommodate the Scots, but there is no reason why one independent state should give way to another. The hope that a common sovereign would do so underestimated the influence of the English parliament and of the city of London. Only an absolute monarch might have been able to overrule them and there was no such being by the late eighteenth century.

The Darien Scheme drew attention to a problem which had been building up as the Scots traded with English colonies, particularly as the pattern of foreign trade moved from being chiefly European to being increasingly American and West Indian. The restrictions of the English Navigation Acts did not always work to Scotland's detriment. They could be circumvented by trading through an English port, and there was also a flourishing illicit trade with the plantations, helped by the presence in them of many Scottish servants, who, with victuals and horses, were exempt from the restrictions. There was, however, a limit to the toleration. So it was with the Darien Scheme which was seen as a direct challenge to the exclusive privileges of the English colonies. The Scots were thought to be going too far and expecting too much. The colonial trade was the most dramatic example of failure to recognise the convergence of interests and of the need to co-operate to resolve any conflict, but ultimately more basic, though it had a less powerful emotional effect, was the effect any protectionist policy could have on the steady growth of direct trade with England, especially in linen and cattle.

In these conditions the economic relations of Scotland and England gave rise to problems, which bear an intriguing resemblance to many of the present-day. The pattern of trade was drawing the two together and, since England was the larger and more powerful neighbour, with control of access to desirable markets at home and abroad, it was difficult for the Scots to maintain independent economic policies if they conflicted with English interests. To have expected any greater co-operation from the English was to show a degree of naivety, which, regrettably, as it may be, has often been a characteristic of the Scots. An alternative was to accept the priority of independent policies even if they harmed the economy; to accept, in the language of the eighteenth century, that political independence was more important than opulence. At times the Scots may have been ready to sacrifice their economic objectives for political ones but by the late seventeenth century it is doubtful – emotional protests to the contrary – if the Scots were willing or able to accept the sacrifices required by English protectionism. A threat to stop imports of linen and cattle from Scotland to England in 1705 was an effective weapon in forcing the Scots to negotiate for union. In a different field, however, the Scots soon found that they had a strong bargaining counter and that was over the succession to the throne, especially after the death of Anne's children. The old dynastic factor came into play. How to cajole or force the Scots into accepting a closer union became a consistent feature in all the variations of English policy towards Scotland until 1707. The Scots may not have been too enthusiastic about a Stewart monarch but it was a risk the English could not dismiss lightly. Each country had a set of counters to play in any moves towards parliamentary union.

The exact details of how the parliamentary union was brought to fruition is a fertile source of disagreement among historians, to a large extent because it is a complex matter. Personal interests played a large part and they were fostered by appropriate bribes and by high hopes of future preferment. It then becomes possible to portray certain of the key figures as virtuous and others as wicked, though the classification is often made by applying the standards of the twentieth century instead of those of the eighteenth. Also, since the various alternatives to an incorporating union were little considered, historians can regret what might have been. In such discussion it is not always clear whether alternatives suggested by latter-day protagonists in the debate were politically acceptable at the time to both parties or whether they were defensible options only over a short and not over a long period of time. If such options were not generally acceptable at the time, it is possible to express regret that the alternative opportunities were lost; to do more is to miss the strength of the forces making for an incorporating union. The Scots had enjoyed a measure of freedom since the Restoration and, with the old festering sore of the ecclesiastical settlement removed, the Scottish parliament wanted to exert its independence, but the disputes over the Navigation Acts, protectionism, colonial policy, culminating in the disaster of Darien, and the increasing importance of English markets for key exports, showed that it was not possible to expand economically without English co-operation. In retrospect it is difficult to understand how the Scots could ever have achieved their desired economic objective independently but that was hardly a live issue. The Scots wanted the economic advantages of association with England, even though they wanted little else from the partnership. The voting figures on the various articles of the Treaty of Union underline its economic attractiveness to the Scots, even if nothing else attracted them. Only 17 voted against Article IV, which offered freedom of trade, though 154 were in favour, but 69 voted against the Treaty as a whole and only 110 in favour. On the other hand, economic concessions were those the English were least likely to surrender but they were a useful prize or bait to be deployed in the efforts to bring the Scots into line with other objectives of English policy such as the succession to the throne.

In such complex negotiations it has become possible for historians to see a host of influences and to come to conclusions varying from outright condemnation, through accusations of political bribery and corruption and suggestions that England forced the Scots into an unwanted and unnecessary union, to commendation of a wise and generous settlement. The more moderate conclusion that another form of association – perhaps an agreement on the succession in return for commercial concessions – was all that was needed fails to take account of the disputes which had gone before and which were likely to follow. The Union of the Crowns simply had not worked, and, in any case, there was little likelihood that English commercial interests would have surrendered their hard-won privileges to the Scots unless they gained something more permanent than an agreement on the succession. Bribes could buy the votes of a few influential figures but not all. A stable and permanent association was needed.

Economic aspects were by no means the only topics that were of concern in the negotiations for union but paying particular attention to them is justified if the historical evidence is to be used to shed light on some of the issues of the present day when economic prospects frequently dominate the discussion. By the late seventeenth century the Scots were becoming more and more integrated into an expanding international economy. That was where their economic future lay so they were vulnerable to any restrictions. To have retreated to reliance on the resources of a closed economy would have spelt continued economic backwardness; to have continued to try to expand unilaterally would have been to encounter the conflicts of the Darien Scheme and threatened the closure of key markets in England and her colonies. The Union of 1707 had flaws and, though reached by agreement, it was not embraced by either party with conspicuous enthusiasm.

Though an incorporating union, there were some fundamental exceptions to its general underlying principle, which had long-term consequences by ensuring the perpetuation of uniquely Scottish institutions. The exceptions were adopted because they enabled some contentious issues to be side-stepped but, somewhat paradoxically, they were to assist the fragmentation of the Union in years to come by providing convenient rallying points for calls for more concessions still. The exceptions followed from the Union of 1707 being by agreement, however forced, and not by conquest or colonisation. The concessions were on matters where it was not worthwhile for the English to put pressure on the Scots by bribes or threats and where attempts at uniformity would have been resisted. They were notably in the church and in the law. To ensure the first, with the novelty of two different established churches in one realm, two Acts (one Scottish and one English) were passed to guarantee the maintenance of each as a 'fundamentall and essentiall Condition of any Treaty'. Presbyterianism was therefore guaranteed in Scotland, a pre-requisite to any successful conclusion of a Treaty, as Defoe recognised when he pointed out that 'if you will form anything here it must be by the ministers'. Similar, though less strict, provisions were made for a separate body of law dealing with private rights which had to remain unaltered 'except for evident utility of the subjects within Scotland', and a distinct judicial system. The exceptions have been maintained, probably more stringently in the case of the church than of the law when appeals went from the Court of Session to the House of Lords, usually with a majority of English judges, and when an increasing body of public law and of welfare provisions led to a common statutory basis for much law in any case.

Both exceptions were recognised by some contemporaries as anomalies which could not be expected to last. The provision for two established churches was held to be 'unpresedented and...so cannot be thought to stand long in Brittain'. As for the law, Lord Hardwicke wrote to Lord Kames that without a common system of law in the two kingdoms 'an incorporating Union would be very defective'. How exceptional these provisions were in an incorporating union is evident by comparison with what happened in Wales and Ireland. Both had established Anglican churches from the sixteenth centuries until their disestablishment in Ireland in 1871 and in Wales in 1920, though in neither case could they claim allegiance from most of the people. So too with the law. While Ireland was not fully integrated into the English legal and administrative system as Wales was, and was not part of the UK until 1801, it had to adopt English law. To try to establish a common established church or law in 1707 was unthinkable but these anomalies in an incorporating union left nuclei of a continuing Scottish identity even for those who had no other form of adherence to the church or direct knowledge of, or interest in, the law.

A union which was less than complete than it would have been if reached by conquest or colonisation, with anomalies left to perpetuate a separate identity, and accepted reluctantly, hardly promised a foundation for future accord, whatever the benefits, actual or potential. To worsen matters any benefits were not evident at once and the Scots were only too well aware of the defects, especially of the burdens of increased taxation. In 1707 the finances of Scotland were in chaos. The stricter financial discipline which followed was unwelcome, especially when it led to the application of techniques and expertise of English officials. The Scots were aware of new and increased taxes and of the absence of those fiscal and economic benefits which had been one of the few attractions of the Union to them. Ecclesiastically, the restoration of the right to appoint parish ministers to lay patrons in 1712, while welcomed by those who exercised it, was regarded as an affront by many others. Such changes affected sections of Scottish society differently but all drew attention to the loss of independence.

With so much suspicion around, and formal recognition of institutions in which it was easy for Scottish sentiment to grow, the question arises of why the Union came to be accepted. One explanation is to hold that the acceptance came from the anglicisation of Scotland, in two ways in particular. The first is straightforward. It is the way in which so many of those in the upper rungs of Scottish society – the peerage and the larger landowners – were assimilated to English ways quickly, by education, marriage, political interests and residence. By descent they were Scots but in social, political and increasingly in ecclesiastical outlook, they were no different from those of comparable standing in England, except perhaps in the relative poverty of many of them. The second influence was more complex. Most of those who stress its effects assume that prior to the Union Scotland was a backward, unenlightened country, dominated in so many fields by obscurantist ministers, and that the Union with England brought the country into much needed contact with a superior culture. Not surprisingly, this interpretation usually gives rise to a good deal of resentment at the arrogance of those who suggest it, so that a grain of truth in what is alleged is easily lost. The weakness of the case is its assumption that Scotland was backward and unenlightened before the Union. It was not. However, the intellectual achievements of Scotland in the eighteenth century were part of a wider European movement, in which Scots took not merely a supporting but often an initiatory role. Those who did so had a Scottish background but they had no strong interest in safeguarding their Scottish identity from being absorbed in a wider European culture. This was evident in their desire to eliminate Scotticisms from their writing and speech. It was given a more serious justification in Adam Smith's warning to the editors of the first *Edinburgh Review* that they would not succeed in their declared objective of demonstrating the advance of science if they stuck to their plan of giving accounts chiefly of books published in Scotland. Perhaps more than any others the intellectual Scots of the eighteenth century were thoroughly internationalist in their outlook, while still living and working in Scotland, and, unlike Boswell, seeing many defects of residence in England.

It is possible to suggest that these characteristics were confined to a powerful elite but it was the influential one at the time. There is a more favourable interpretation to keep in mind. Even the apparent social snobbery had the effect of trying to move Scottish society from introverted isolation to concern with its role and image on a wider front. To encourage the reverse would have led to increased parochial isolationism, which is always fatally attractive in small countries such as Scotland, especially if they feel overwhelmed by a more powerful neighbour. Ireland's relations with Great Britain is an example, and, within Ireland, those of Northern Ireland to the Republic.

Cultural assimilation did take place but there were some, even among the elite, who remained at home to improve their estates and the country more generally. To them, the economic success of the Union was to commend it in time. That success came with the expansion of trade, initially on the basis of the protection offered by inclusion within the English Navigation Acts, and best illustrated by the growth of the tobacco trade and the commercial expansion of Glasgow. In due course the city moved to become the centre of the industrial complex of west-central Scotland and that too was a success based on the wider markets of England, the Empire and the world. The industrial success of Scotland, initially as part of the customs union of Great Britain and latterly in an increasingly free-trade international economy, is well-known and calls for no elucidation.

The period of internationalism and acceptance of the Union began to change from the late nineteenth century but it was only in the twentieth century, and increasingly in its second half, that serious criticism mounted. The challenge came from an increasingly introverted perspective on Scottish life and its external relations which is evident in two major directions.

The first is in some significant changes in cultural attitudes which stressed the distinctiveness of Scottish life and culture. The institutions left at the Union and their practitioners remained to assert their own distinctiveness and to influence others. Scottish lawyers, even more than Scottish ministers, are tied to practising in Scotland and so incline to be more insular in outlook than is the case in other professions, though the insularism has been dented by the wider implications of commercial law and the pressures of the European Community. A contrast which highlights the professional isolation of the lawyers is with the accountants. Though merger with their English equivalent has been resisted, the linkages between the accountants' institutes are so great that professional issues are decided jointly. The isolationism of the legal profession has been heightened by its tightly-knit community in Edinburgh centred on the Faculty of Advocates, the members of which for generations have been able to exercise a degree of influence over Scottish affairs out of all proportion to their numbers. Of more general influence is the Church of

Scotland which, though now a minority interest, still asserts a right to be heard as speaking for the whole of Scotland. The Church is ready to advance its views, particularly through its Church and Nation Committee, on a wide range of issues which, however, it usually does from a narrow Scottish standpoint with inadequate recognition of the fact that, whether it likes it or not, Scotland is part of the UK. Subtly the move is made to a perception that everything should be judged from a constitutional position which does not exist.

Stress on Scottish distinctiveness did not necessarily lead to any suggestion that there should be political change; sometimes it was even the reverse. The stress on a distinctive Scottish life but within a unionist state was spread widely by the romantic movement in the hands of Scott, but modern Scottish literature has adopted a different approach. The rejection of the kailyard writers of the late nineteenth century gave rise to a literary genre which was infused with political attitudes which were left-wing and nationalist. It not only encouraged many to think that a separate Scottish identity was being lost, but that it was being submerged, either deliberately or by neglect by a political culture which was at variance with that of Scotland. Some of the historical basis for Scottish distinctiveness was unreliable, but that does not detract from the powerful influence of the movement. It encouraged the clutter of symbolism, which the tourist trade soon fostered, and which, for good, bad, right or wrong reasons, draws attention to the alleged differences of Scotland, so that a Gaelic-speaking Highland ancestry was attributed to many Scots, many of whom have known nothing but life in the urban, industrial belt since their ancestors came from Ireland.

The emphasis on distinctiveness has grown since 1945 in many walks of life, some trivial, others less so. There is an aggressive assertion of Scottish achievements in sport, whether worthwhile or not, with demands for separate representation and separate national anthems; demands for the retention of Scottish regiments have produced some unlikely alliances; the saltire and the lion rampant are flown increasingly instead of the Union flag by those whose knowledge of heraldic symbolism is non-existent. At a more serious level almost every organisation now deems it must be organised separately in Scotland whether there is any good reason for doing so or not; an obligation is canvassed widely to give preferential support to Scottish products and services, even by some to the extent that they would pay more for them.

The stress on Scottish distinctiveness encourages constitutional distinctiveness as well, often unwittingly. If separate Scottish identity is to be found in so many fields, its absence in constitutional matters becomes increasingly obvious, and so increasingly anomalous to many. The background of distinctiveness – of whatever kind – has meant that it became easy to assume, without any direct attention to its ramifications, that there should be constitutional distinctiveness as well.

Second, and perhaps of greater significance in criticism of the Union since 1945, is the decline of the economic success which had been such a potent force behind the internationalism which had welcomed the Union. It was a decline in which Scottish experience was not so very different from that of the UK as a whole. The UK was becoming less competitive and Scotland with it. Until the First World War the adverse consequences of the changing international economy were not evident. Indeed, some were beneficial, as were the cheaper foodstuffs which became available and which did not have the same adverse effects on Scottish agriculture as they did in the more arable areas of England. There were certainly changes which gave rise to indicators of industrial decline before 1914 but their serious harmful consequences lay in the future. Examples were in the increased dependence on specialist industrial production, some of which – notably the demand for warships – depended on circumstances which would not last, and on the exploitation of exhaustible reserves of coal for export. After 1918 the decline of Scottish economic success could not be ignored. In retrospect the change does not seem so sudden as it did to contemporaries, and to understand some of their responses to the changed circumstances it is necessary to stress how surprising and unexpected the change was to them, especially in Glasgow and the west of Scotland which had been the centre of the earlier economic success and where there had grown up a dangerous belief in the impregnable skill and ability of the workforce and a complacency in their achievements. In these conditions it was easy to fear that, if something was wrong in the economy, the fault lay with someone else.

Economic dissatisfaction lent support to political independence in the twentieth century with the growth of intervention by the state in social and latterly in economic life. After 1945 there was general acceptance that government could and should avoid or offset the adverse consequences of economic decline, a view which was encouraged still further when politicians claimed to be able to provide economic improvements with a confidence exceeding anything shown by their predecessors. This was an approach which fitted well with much Scottish political sentiment, which was often more interventionist than in the rest of the UK, and remained so even when such views faded elsewhere, so providing a marked contrast from the conventional view of a rugged Scottish individualism. The outcome was that both the elected and the electorate came to believe after 1945 that it was within their power to effect an economic transformation, if not a miracle. When, at the same time, there was an increasing identification of Scotland as a distinct and unique part of the UK, it is easy to draw the conclusion that separate constitutional arrangements for Scotland would provide freedom to adopt the most appropriate economic policies. The move in this direction was encouraged by the increased administrative devolution of power to the Scottish Office and other Scottish agencies and the accompanying availability of material, especially statistical and other information in a Scottish form. Problems and solutions were seen more and more exclusively as uniquely Scottish and so often in a political and constitutional context which did not exist. It is not unrealistic to suggest that, paradoxically, to devolve more and more power on a Scottish base as a means of preserving the Union is to ensure that it becomes more fragmented and so more unstable. As so many aspects of Scottish life are split off in independent organisations, often for no other reasons than the desire to have a Scottish unit, then at some stage the forces of isolationism take over from those of internationalism, and so reverse the process initiated in the eighteenth century.

And, at a personal level, there is always the fatal attraction to many in a small country of being big fish even in a small pond.

Any argument against the powerful strength of this isolationist force is likely to be underestimated or even neglected. In the current discussion it is rare to find any consideration of the present over-representation of Scotland at Westminster or on how proposed constitutional arrangements may affect the powers of Scottish MPs in the future. Only the emergence of some political forces working in the opposite direction might arrest the drift towards fragmentation of the Union and in recent years it would seem that they have worked in the opposite direction. One was the decline in Liberal Unionism, which had been a potent force in the west of Scotland where the links with Northern Ireland ensured strong Scottish support for Unionism. Another was the changing balance within the Labour party in favour of a less integrated union. As the fear of nationalism in any form faded with the decline in the ideals of international socialism, the possibility that a break in the Union would deliver political power to the left more rapidly in Scotland than in the UK seemed attractive. The implications of such changes in the numbers and the nature or the representation at Westminster were hardly taken into account, even when a Labour majority at Westminster depended on the Scottish members or when the leadership of the party was in Scottish hands.

A historian has no special competence in looking to the future but a survey of the past suggests that the isolationist tendencies of the Scots, which have grown this century, may have taken on such momentum that they will now be satisfied only by total independence. It may seem defensible to proceed along that path given the declared objectives of many critics. The danger in doing so is that it will lead to an end which many, if not most, do not want. A survey of the past shows why it is also one fraught with obstacles. The integration of centuries cannot be put aside lightly. There would be fearsome problems in separation and no guarantee that independence for Scotland will avoid the difficulties which led to its end three hundred years ago. Critics of the Union fail to recognise adequately how devolution of powers to Scotland alone and not as part of a wholesale restructuring of the government of the UK will lead to still more calls for greater and greater independence. If stress on Scottish distinctiveness is extended to embrace constitutional distinctiveness, then the Union is unlikely to survive. The challenge is how to retain a separate Scottish identity but with a political structure that is totally integrated with that in other parts of the UK.

The English, the Scots and the British

John Morrill

The Union of England and Scotland in 1707 was a kind of shotgun marriage; but in many ways it was the English rather than the Scots who felt trapped into it. For at least 150 years it was the Scots who had been striving to put the relationship of the two kingdoms onto a more formal and stable basis and the English who were content to leave things as they were, in an informal relationship in which the English commanded and the Scots found themselves dragged along.

It is simply not the case that the English ruthlessly and cynically took over Scotland by a crude combination of bribes and bullying. Seen in the context of the early modern period as a whole it was neither inevitable nor unexpected. It was of a piece with processes of historical development that were commonplace in a European context and part of the process of creation of the multinational states that were *and are* the norm. Scottish aspirants to an historically-validated independence from the British state are whistling in the wind.

For four hundred years after the Norman Conquest, the English monarchy had been preoccupied with establishing itself as a cross-Channel Norman/Angevin Empire and had only spasmodically looked north and west. Two and a half things changed this in the century after 1453. The first was the complete defeat of English kings in France and their expulsion from the continent, which made them look long and hard at the prospects of expanding their power within the British archipelago. The second was the fact of the Reformation which created such seismic insecurities throughout Christendom. Everywhere rulers strove to impose religious uniformity throughout their dominions, and confessional divides caused them to fear and suspect close neighbours.

As far as Anglo-Scottish relations were concerned, centuries of sparring about whether or not the northern kingdom owed feudal fealty to the southern kingdom (a claim which dominated English policy following the death of James V as Henry strove to control the wardship and marriage of his daughter and heiress) was accompanied from 1502 by a game of dynastic roulette with the marriage of Henry VII's elder daughter to the King of Scots. This gave rise to the tantalizing prospect of a fusion of the royal houses, something which finally came to pass in 1603. Henry VIII's complex marital relations, which meant that he died leaving a sickly boy as his heir and two daughters both bastards in English law and the second manifestly a bastard in the eyes of the international catholic community, added piquancy to this dynastic dimension to the British problem.

The early modern period saw throughout Europe the rise of the multiple or composite monarchies. For England, Scotland, Ireland (resulting in the UK), read France, Brittany, Burgundy (resulting in France) or Castile, Aragon, Catalonia (resulting in Spain); and there was a comparable process elsewhere which produced a series of central and northern European composite states. If there was anything odd about the 'British' experience, it was the creation of an archipelagic composite state rather than a territorially contiguous one.

Within the British archipelago two processes can be seen as happening simultaneously: the core areas of England, Scotland, Ireland and Wales all began to absorb and integrate their peripheral regions to create four 'nations' for the first time; and the English core began to exercise greater authority over the outlying cores.

The four 'cores' were lowland regions where the language, social institutions (feudal patterns of landholding and inheritance) and legal codes and practices derived from the Normans and had evolved in parallel with one another; each being set against peripheral highland, forest or waterlogged areas marked by linguistic, social and legal divergence. Indeed insofar as 'Scotland' existed as an effective political entity its heartland was precisely in that area that drew its language, law, social norms and religious culture from the same Norman taproot as lowland England. Did Celtic Scots see themselves as 'Scots' as against often rather remote and grudging subjects of the king of Scotland? Nor must we forget the Macdonald Lordship of the Isles, almost as autonomous from Scotland as Scotland was of England.

In England, as in Scotland, the main thrust of the sixteenth century was the creation of a unitary state, with the final triumph of writ culture, primogeniture, a royal monopoly of political violence throughout the 'realm'. One can see the same process working miraculously and effectively throughout Wales and succeeding institutionally but not culturally in Ireland. By 1600, the inhabitants of Scotland were more of a people than ever before; Scottish law and Scottish Protestantism were making rapid progress in Gaelic-speaking areas; and Scotland was for the first time becoming a geopolitical as well as a geographical reality in the same way as England, Wales and Ireland were becoming more meaningful geopolitical realities. For between 1534 and 1547 the Tudor realms had been transformed in theory and practice by parliamentary acts of union and unification whose first purpose was to assimilate them to lowland English customs and laws and only secondarily to redefine the relationship of an integrated principality of Wales and kingdom (in place of the medieval lordship) of Ireland. By 1600 there were four kingdoms/principalities in an uncertain relationship one to another but all more self-consciously integrated within themselves than they had been in previous centuries.

Sixteenth-century Scots were more conscious of the archipelagic implications of these changes than the English were. They had either fought against their likely destiny or they had embraced it with varying degrees of distaste. The nation had been traumatized first in 1513 by seeing one quarter of its greater nobility slaughtered at Flodden and their king's body carted off to London and denied Christian burial; and then in the 1540s by the further military humiliations of Solway Moss and Pinkie and by the vicious cruelty of Henry VIII's Rough Wooing (his recognition of the sixteenth-century equivalent of the Geneva Conventions always stopped at the English border). This induced an inferiority complex – perhaps given the respective sizes, comparative wealth and populations, one might say it induced a sense of reality – that recognized that Scotland's destiny lay in acknowledging and coming to terms with England or seeking union with a major European power. In effect this meant recognizing that Mary Queen of Scots should either marry Edward Prince of Wales or Francis, Dauphin of France. It is striking that those struggling to control the government of the infant queen were not concerned merely to tie Scotland to the royal families of England or France, but to the heirs to the thrones of these states. In that gendered age, that meant offering Scotland as a junior title to the royal houses of England or France. Let us just consider what would have happened if Francis II had not died of an ear infection at the age of 18 before he could impregnate Mary. Any son of that union would have been heir to France, Scotland and England. How independent would Scotland have been then?

In the event, the French overplayed their hand, and their aspiration for turning Scotland into a colonial dependency of France was all too evident from the ominous number of military and legal 'advisers' flooding into Scotland even before Mary signed away her rights as Queen to her husband at her marriage. Those with short memories and those drawn to the Protestant religion turned from 1558 to the new Queen of England. We must never forget that in 1560 Elizabeth responded to the pleas for assistance from the Lords of the Congregation and that the English played a crucial part in driving out the French *and then withdrew themselves*. In the period 1560-1603 the English Queen consistently refused to intrude herself in the internal affairs of Scotland, despite the pleas of successive Regents – for example the Earl of Morton's call for a 'conformity of Kirks' in the 1570s. Elizabeth refused to allow her Bishops to interfere in the disputes within the Kirk. Meanwhile a principal influence on the shape of the Scottish Church was the fact that its intellectual and clerical leadership for at least a generation was formed by men whose Protestantism had been matured in exile in England during the reign of Edward VI and in exile with the English in Germany and Switzerland in the mid-1550s. The Book of Common Order was the prayer book of the *English* exiles. Although the English drifted back from the austere forms of the 1550s, the Scots retained them, and spent much of the later sixteenth century calling the English back to them. As Arthur Williamson (1979: pp 1-48) has shown, there was a strong element within the Kirk looking forward to the Union of the Crowns because it would bring about a *British* apocalypse. In the later sixteenth century it was the Scots, not the English, who devoted most thought and effort to the necessity and hazards of the Stewart inheritance of the southern Crowns. Apprehensive, unenthusiastic, but realistic, it was the Scots who would spend the seventeenth century embracing the unavoidability of the Union and seeking to find a way of giving it an institutional coherence.

II

From the arrival of James VI on the English throne, the English tried to prevent the Union of the Crowns turning into a Union of the Kingdoms. James himself had worked out a gradualist programme that would begin with creating a 'union of hearts and minds' (Galloway 1986: p 165) and would proceed via common citizenship, free trade and a mingling of elites through intermarriage to a union of laws and finally – eventually – to a union of political and religious institutions. James probably did not expect to get to that 'perfect union' during his own lifetime; but he certainly expected to get further than he did, and the main cause of the failure to progress was the absolute refusal of the English political elite gathered in Parliament to contemplate any enhancement of the rights of Scotsmen in England. Some would begrudgingly consider an *'incorporative'* union on the model of the Tudor incorporation of Wales into a Greater English state, but James's 'perfect union' – in the sense of supra-national institutions and legal systems – held no attractions for the English, and free trade and common citizenship seemed to them to convey great benefits to the Scots and none to the English (Galloway 1986: pp 161-75; Levack 1987: pp 31-51). It is a striking fact about the seventeenth century that no Englishmen became major landowners in Scotland (even under the Cromwellian incorporative union); no English families snapped up the heiresses to great Scottish estates and although a significant number of Scottish earls took English brides (Brown 1990), no English earls took Scottish brides.

Over the first forty years of the Union of the Crowns the English found that a politics of neglect served them well enough as far as Scotland was concerned. They might plan a rolling programme of confiscation and plantation of Irish land; they might ensure that an English-dominated British Council in Whitehall constructed a foreign and commercial policy indifferent (and at times damaging) to Scottish interests; they might come to tolerate a strong Scottish presence in the royal household (a presence with unquantifiable influence over policy and patronage in all three kingdoms); but there was no apparent interest in any constitutional rearrangement of Britain. For example no archbishop resurrected the ancient claims of the English metropolitans to ecclesiastical supremacy within a British Patriarchy (Morrill 1994). Despite James's promotion of 'Britishness' on his coins, seals, and flag, the notion did not catch on. I can find no Englishman calling himself 'British' before the 1640s, whereas those amphibious Scots who held large estates in Scotland and prominent positions at the court (together with earldoms in both countries) did refer themselves in petitions to Charles as 'we your Majesty's British nobility' (Cowan 1980: p 131).

But the Scots had every reason to be unhappy, especially after the accession of Charles I. Charles had no vision of union. He was an authoritarian king, set on maximizing his power in each of his kingdoms in accordance with what he took to be his rights in each. There were common elements in his authoritarianism – such as his attempt to restore to the Churches of England, Ireland and Scotland much of the land plundered from them at the Reformation – but on the whole it is a *style* of government, not common policies let alone a drive to create a single monarchy out of his composite monarchy, which caused the reaction that brought civil war to all three kingdoms and complex patterns of alliances and war between them. Charles's Scottish Act of Revocation by which he sought to rearrange the terms on which grants of former crown and church land were held had no parallel in England; and the striking thing about the canons and prayer book which he sought to impose on the Scots in the 1630s was not that they were anglicising (or anglicanising) measures but that they sought to impose religious observances after the king's own heart not after the practice of the Church of England. He did not seek to impose the English canons of 1604 of the English prayer book, but ones designed for what the King (often ignorantly) took to be Scottish conditions (Morrill 1994: pp 231-36).

Charles's attempt – without consulting a General Assembly, a Parliament, the Scottish Council (or even the Scottish Bishops in conclave) – to impose a new liturgy led the greater part of the Scottish nation to covenant together to protect their Reformation and their rule of law. Charles's attempts to use the resources of the whole of the British Isles to impose his will on his Scottish subjects led to the Scottish invasion of England, the calling of the Long Parliament and the collapse of both Ireland and England into civil war. The years 1641-1651 must be seen first and foremost as the war of the three kingdoms, with Scottish troops in Ireland as well as England, and with a king who constantly thought three-dimensionally, seeking to use the resources of each kingdom for the restoration of his power throughout the archipelago (Morrill 1993: pp 96-102).

The point I need to make here is that the Scots but not the English Parliamentarians and Regicides believed that the structural instabilities of the composite British monarchy made a post-war constitutional reorganisation and federal union not only desirable but essential. From not later than the winter of 1639-40 the Covenanters were fighting not simply or principally to nurture Scottish liberties under a Scottish king, but for a federal union of the three kingdoms and three churches. They had recognized that there would be no protection for Scotland against a king willing to mobilize the resources of the three kingdoms unless he was equally constrained in all kingdoms. Having in 1639-40 inflicted the first important Scots defeat on an English army for over 300 years, they made a common form of church government and confession of faith, along with political structures designed to co-ordinate policy-making and legislation in the two kingdoms, a prime objective of the subsequent peace negotiations. They also assumed that the Irish Church would be reformed along identical lines and that the Scots would be accorded an active role in the affairs of Ireland. As we will see, they were continually rebuffed by the English Parliament, but they were ever more determined that there could be no settlement other than an archipelagic one. It was this which brought the Covenanters into the war in Ireland in 1642 and in England in 1643. The Solemn League and Covenant is an agreement covering all three kingdoms and requiring changes in the government and religion of all three. The outcome the Scots sought was a federal union with separate political, legal and ecclesiastical institutions in each but a high degree of congruity and co-operation between them. This is most dramatically illustrated by the West-minster Assembly, the meeting of English and Scots ministers and lay assessors which met to design a system of church government and discipline, confession of faith, catechism and service book which would be introduced into the independent churches of England, Scotland and Ireland. The Scots were massively outnumbered at that assembly, but bound themselves to accept its decisions, although it would involve changes in the Kirk. Hence their rage when the English Parliament chopped and changed what had been agreed in the assembly without any reference to them.

The disillusionment of the Covenanting leadership with the English was concerned with a whole range of archipelagic (and not just British) issues: the dishonouring of agreements to provide for the Scottish Army in Ireland; the establishing of a new Lord Lieutenant to undertake an English recon-quest of Ireland in defiance of promises that it would be an archipelagic undertaking; the standing down of the Committee of Both Kingdoms, the only co-ordinating body created in the war years; and the continuing indif-ference of the English to Scots demands for the appointment of *conservatores pacis* or other joint bodies of parliamentary commissioners and councillors from the two kingdoms. No wonder many lukewarm supporters of the Solemn League transferred their hopes for a federal unionist future from an alliance with the Long Parliament to an alliance with a hopefully chastened and wiser king.

Nothing illustrates more dramatically the unswerving commitment of the Covenanting leadership to federal unionism, to a single historical destiny, than their response to the trial and execution of Charles I. On the very day that news of the regicide reached Scotland, Charles II was proclaimed king of Great Britain and Ireland in Edinburgh, and less than two years later he swore, again as king of Great Britain and Ireland, to introduce the Covenants into all his kingdoms. If the Scots had proclaimed Charles as king of Scotland but not of England and Ireland, the chances are they would have been left alone by the English Parliament and Army. It was because they saw no historical security or destiny for themselves outside a Union that the Scots proclaimed Charles king of Britain and mobilized themselves once more for a third and fateful British war.

Nonetheless I have already implied that there were those at the time who were single-minded in seeing the affairs of Scotland and Ireland as at best a noisome intrusion into English affairs, to be pushed out of sight and as far as possible out of mind. I am referring to the very army grandees and Long Parliament leaders whose little-Englander attitudes drove the Covenanters to distraction. The hallmarks of men like Viscount Saye and the earl of Northumberland in the Lords and Pym and later St. John and Cromwell in the Commons was a desire to use Scots military muscle to defeat the king of England, but not to honour any political (let alone religious) agreements with them that created any kind of federal union; and a refusal to find out about the complexities of Irish political culture. Ireland was to be conquered and raped, and a policy of religious apartheid developed to justify the mass expropriation of the native peoples. To complete the picture they were determined to deny the rights of the Scots to any involvement in the government of post-conquest Ireland.

Their view was certainly not a holistic one. In 1640, these men were willing to barter with Charles: he could have the funds to raise a major royal army against the Covenanters if they could have grievances settled. In 1641 they were grateful to the Scots for ensuring a long parliament but they stalled every attempt to negotiate clause 8 of the Treaty of London which would have redefined the relationship of the Kingdoms. It set the pattern for the years that followed. The terms of the Solemn League and Covenant were only taken seriously by the English so far as they advanced military victory and as soon as that was accomplished the Parliament did two things which showed its true feelings: it stood down the Committee of Both Kingdoms and it appointed a new Lord Lieutenant for Ireland with a remit that excluded the Scots.

Perhaps even more telling, however, was what happened when such actions and the emasculation of the accords of the Westminster Assembly and the proclamation of a measure of religous liberty drove the Scots into an alliance with Charles I. For once Cromwell and the New Model Army had defeated the Scots, they showed little interest in conquering Scotland or in incorporating it into a British state. They delightedly withdrew as soon as Argyll and his faction staged a coup in Edinburgh. 'I do think the affairs of Scotland are in a thriving condition as to the interest of honest men ... although our brothers in Scotland were our greatest enemies, God has justified us in their sight; caused us to requite good for evil, causing them to acknowledge it publicly by acts of state, and privately.' Conquest, he continued, 'was not unfeasible, but I think not Christian' (Abbott 1937-1947: I, p 677). As David Stevenson (1990: p 154) has put it: 'By requiting evil with good, Cromwell hoped he had put the Scots under the unbreakable moral obligation to live in friendship with England'. The English had no interest in Scotland so long as it posed no threat to England. When they executed Charles I (Charles I of Scotland remember) they abolished monarchy in England and Ireland but were silent about Scotland. As far as they were concerned the union of the crowns had been severed and Scotland was free to go along its own line as a free independent state. As Portugal had been united to Spain in 1580 and resumed its own separate historical path in 1640, so Scotland was now free to go its own way.

The Little Englander politicians and generals who executed Charles were thus stunned and disoriented when the Scottish executive (on 5th February 1649, the very day that news reached Edinburgh) proclaimed Charles II as 'King of Great Britain, France and Ireland', and when the Scots went on in due course to crown Charles at Scone with a solemn oath to give his assent to acts to be passed 'enjoining (the Covenants) in my other dominions' (Charles II 1651: p 40). Only this forced the English into reluctant conquest and incorporative union with its northern protestant neighbour. What is amazing is the lack of intellectual fervour, enthusiasm, curiosity about the process of absorption, and the indifference in England to sustaining it beyond 1660. The Unions of the 1650s involved the English in a sort of shotgun bigamy.

At first sight the 1650s are uniquely a period when the assertion of Britishness is essential to an understanding of the historical process. For the only time before 1801 there was a single legislature for the whole of the Britannic archipelago, and a greater degree of administrative and judicial centralisation. The general elections of 1654, 1656 and 1659 saw the return of 30 MPs for Scotland and Ireland; there was a single Council of State/Privy Council based in Whitehall with counsellors or commissioners in Edinburgh and Dublin whose independence resembled that of the pre-war Councils in the North and in the Marches of Wales far more than it resembled that of the pre-war royal Councils of Scotland and Ireland. The degree of military integration under the Lord General Cromwell was also greater than at any other period. Certainly it is not possible to write Scottish or Irish history at this time except in a Britannic context: of unprecedented English intervention, control and acculturation. Although there was no English colonisation of Scotland in the 1650s, there was a systematic attempt to change the social basis of power away from the established nobility with the creation of a strong autonomous class of small proprietors who were responsive to the anglicisation of Scottish law and government. Furthermore, the commissioners for the administration of justice in Scotland were to be predominantly English and their task was to impose English civil law on the Scots and assimilate Scottish criminal law to English process and substance.

And yet even in the 1650s the situation is not straightforward. Viewed from an English perspective there was considerable lack of enthusiasm for and interest in the union of the three ex-kingdoms. No-one came up with a new name for the new polity: the Instrument of Government provides a paper constitution for 'the Commonwealth of England, Scotland and Ireland'; and neither the constitutional bill of the first Protectorate Parliament nor the Humble Petition and Advice modified that style. The union of Parliaments was a legal fiction, the electoral provision for Scotland and Ireland being principally intended to ensure the return of representatives of the garrisons and of English colonial administrators; while the legislative record of the parliaments of the 1650s shows little concern either to make special provision for the needs of Scotland and Ireland, or to take account of conditions or custom there in the framing of legislation. If Union meant free trade for the Scots and for Irish Protestants, it did not mean fiscal equality; successive regimes taxing England hard, but Scotland and Ireland much harder. No wonder Robert Blair could write that 'as for the embodying of Scotland with England, it will be as when the poor bird is embodied into the hawk that hath eaten it up' (McCrie 1842: p 292)

At the Restoration, no-one sought to perpetuate the Cromwellian Union. The constitutional relationship reverted to one of separate kingdoms until a single king. The Scots nobility stayed more at home licking their wounds and kicking their tenants; Charles II's lazy pragmatism laced with periodic vindictiveness against the field conventicles produced a political system of benign indulgence of noble power designed to ensure that the defence of Scotland was not a charge to the English Exchequer .

With James VII and II, as with Charles I (whose faults and blindnesses he redoubled), each of the British monarchies experienced its own raw authoritarianism; and each responded by acts of repudiation that were distinctively its own. Once more the English were indifferent to the constitutional implications for the whole of the transfer of sovereignty from James to his daughter and son-in-law. Although a few voices in Scotland called for a federal union in 1689, they were little heeded, and the English were indifferent both to those calls for union and to the fact that the revolution in Scotland spelt any danger to their self-interest. But in fact the Claim of Right, and more particularly the establishment of a Scottish Parliament in which the Scottish executive no longer held a stranglehold, introduced a significant shift in the relations of the two countries, and it was this shift which brought about the crisis which resulted in the Act of Union of 1707.

It follows from all the foregoing that there was nothing inevitable about the Act of 1707. But for the precise nature of the transfer of sovereignty in 1689, the Scots would not have had any mechanism or leverage to compel the English to negotiate over free trade and other matters; without the failure of each of Anne's seventeen pregnancies to provide an heir to the Stuart thrones, there would have been no political and constitutional crisis to give the Scots Parliament the issue on which to exercise this power of leverage; without the economic collapse of the 1690s and the belief that the English could have prevented or alleviated it, the will to use the leverage might well not have existed. Be all those things as they may, the fact is that there was no political will in Scotland to break the dynastic union, and there was an opportunity to change it to Scots advantage. It was all very well for the Scots in 1703 to assert their right to dispose of the Crown separately from England. It is even clearer now than it was at the time that they had no choice but to opt for the House of Hanover.

Several things were not new in 1706-7. There was nothing new in Scottish recognition that dynastic union was undesirable and had brought more problems than benefits. There was nothing new in Scottish recognition that a union that combined an integrative union of political institutions with important federative principles which preserved Scottish religion and law was preferable to an exposed independence in a tougher world. What was new was the English willingness to concede a limited union. Now the English were willing to barter free trade for the security of incorporating Scottish legislative autonomy into a British Parliament dominated by the English. And they were willing to pay generously for that deal – not just in the greasing of Scottish parliamentary palms but in the binding nature of the guarantees on the Kirk and the legal system, the proportionately excessive number of parliamentary seats at Westminster for Scotland and the terms of the free trade clauses. If the English bought Scotland, the Scots sold themselves dear.

The Union of 1707 was both a logical and balanced outcome to a century of uneasy dynastic union during which the Scots had shown realism and the English had brushed the problems under the carpet. That there might come a time when the English would rue their perpetual short-sightedness and come to an accommodation was a probability. When that might happen; just how that might happen; and what form that further union would take and what each party would gain and lose was neither predictable nor inevitable.

III

Nothing in the foregoing is intended to defend the Union. There may well be good and sufficient reasons for ending it. But it is intended to deny that the Scots were trapped into a union designed to sap Scotland of its own culture and to render it a dependency of the English. In the seventeenth century it was the Scots who sought to create a united kingdom – albeit a federated one that protected the particular religious and legal institutions of the Scottish renaissance – and the English who displayed a calculated and at times callous indifference. My argument has been that the Scots spurned the opportunities to re-establish independence of England for good and rational reasons and that in the end they got more of what they wanted than did the English.

The Union of 1707 made good sense in the context of early modern Britain. If Scotland wants to end its marriage to England, it may have grounds for a divorce on the grounds of mental cruelty, but there are no grounds for an annulment. The marriage itself may have been rather hurried at the end, but it was the considered end of a long courtship, and it was unquestionably a legal and a valid union.

The Union of the kingdoms in 1707, coming a century after the dynastic union, was a benign example of phenomena commonplace in early modern Europe. The kingdom of France was a composite of peoples and dominions for centuries as autonomous one of another as England, Ireland and Scotland – the kingdom of France, the duchies of Brittany (incorporated by inheritance) and of Burgundy (incorporated by conquest), quite apart from the duchies and counties gained from the Anglo-Norman Empire and the Pyrannean princedoms. The kingdom of Spain is a comparable composite created by dynastic chance. And then there were the artificially created Habsburg kingdom of Austria-Hungary, the Hohenzollern kingdom of Prussia, and – at various times – the composite Baltic monarchies.

The consequence – as Hugh Seton-Watson (1977) demonstrated a generation ago – is that the nation-state is the aberrant form in European history, not the norm. Most states are multi-cultural, multi-national entities and few nations are to be found in a single state. Although we wilfully mislead by speaking of the United Nations when we mean the United States of the World, or when we speak of international relations when we mean interstate relations, the fact is Britain is the norm rather than the exception to the rule in containing within it in creative tension peoples with a strong sense of separate historical roots which have become intertwined.

As an historian I am very drawn to the model for understanding the British archipelago developed by John Pocock in an outstanding series of articles launched with a plea for 'British History: a new subject' almost twenty years ago. Pocock has called us to a holistic approach to what he has termed 'the atlantic archipelago', but he insisted that we must adopt a pluralistic approach which recognizes but does not exaggerate the extent to which such a history must contain 'the increasing dominance of England as a political and cultural entity' (Pocock 1975). He went on to say that British History must show how the component parts of these islands '*interacted so as to modify the conditions of one another's existence*', and that 'British history denotes the historiography of no single nation but of a problematic and uncompleted experiment in the creation and interaction of several nations' (Pocock 1982).

I repeat that none of this argues against the possibility that the historical forces that shaped *Britain* have worked themselves through and that there are new countervailing forces – the possibilities of breaking down state structures so as to liberate nations within a new European super-state. I have to say that just as much of what beguiled the English and the Scots into a fixed union in 1707 was contingent and ephemeral, so the factors that make some advocate a 'wider European federalism' as a way forward for a Scotland disconnected from Westminster look to me to be dangerously contingent considerations.

We are heading for the tercentenary of the Union. As a Bill of Rights for the Scots it has stood the test of time quite well. The distinctiveness of Scottish law and religion has never been fundamentally undermined, and both have been reinforced by the evolution of a distinctive Scottish educational system. The English never reneged on their commitments to those aspects of Scottish national identity. Nor did they ever renege on the opening up of English commerce or English colonies to Scots. Both became truly British and the Empire was in fact as well as in name a British Empire.

In that sense the spirit of the Union has remained intrinsic to it. It has left most Scots at most times keenly aware that they had two identities – a Scottish identity and a British identity and Roy Campbell's essay in the present collection ends with an extremely telling analysis of how the sense of Scottish cultural distinctiveness has waxed in modern times just when any sense of constitutional distinctiveness has waned. His final plea is well taken. But it must be confronted that while no Scot would readily conflate and confuse 'Scottish' and 'British' many (most?) English – especially English politicians – do so all the time. If the challenge for the Scots is – as Roy Campbell puts it – how to retain a separate Scottish identity but with a political structure that is totally integrated with that in other parts of the UK, the challenge for the English is to create a political structure that recognizes and draws on the many and increasing cultural identities that constitute Britishness.

Almost three centuries ago Andrew Fletcher of Saltoun, as much a Scottish secular saint as Scottishness will permit, argued against the Union of 1707. It is often forgotten that he was not against union, but against most forms of union, and especially the one on offer. His view was quite clear: so long as England remained England, there was no security for Scotland. It would always be the poor bird embodied in the hawk. The true security of Scotland lay in the break-up of England into a federation of regions – the nearer it came to restoring the Heptarchy the better. Recreate a federal England and Scotland could be added to their number. My suggestion would be that the Scots should not try to disintegrate Britain; nor put their faith in a mega-federation of European states; but work for a radical process of decentralisation that liberates Wales and the English regions even as it liberates Scotland. Andrew Fletcher could yet turn out to be a British prophet (and saint?).

The Union of 1707 and the British Constitution

Colin R Munro

'The Union has been long desired by both Nations, and We shall Esteem it as the greatest Glory of Our Reign to have it now Perfected, being fully perswaded, That it must prove the greatest Happiness of our People.

An intire and perfect Union will be the solid Foundation of lasting Peace; It will secure your Religion, Liberty and Property, remove the Animosities amongst your Selves, and the jealousies and Differences betwixt Our Two Kingdoms: It must increase your Strength, Riches and Trade, and by this Union the whole Island being joyned in Affection and free from all Apprehension of different Interests, will be enabled to Resist all its Enemies, support the Protestant interest everywhere, and maintain the Liberties of Europe.'

(Queen Anne's letter to the Scottish Parliament at the opening of the session on 3 October 1706)

Queen Anne's sentiments were not shared by all of her Scottish subjects. But they were widely enough held amongst the parliamentarians in the Estates for the terms of union to be sanctioned by a clear majority there and, following the English Parliament's assent, the state of Great Britain came into being on 1 May 1707.

The consequences of that Union for Scotland may be contested, and the very circumstances of the Union, nearly three centuries ago, are still debated. Was it a freely negotiated agreement or was it a treaty of surrender obtained by bribery or *force majeure*? In either event, should the Union legislation be regarded as a special constitutional document, or merely as a law like any other? Might it perhaps be re-negotiated? Can it be dissolved?

Calculations of costs and benefits which involve the unbundling of such a long period of common history are not easily made. However, a constitutional lawyer may attempt to answer at least some of the questions concerning the Acts of Union themselves and the constitutional position of Scotland within the UK in the 1990s.

The Union legislation consisted of a principal Act composed of twenty-five Articles, and three associated Acts which provided for the continuance of the different established churches in Scotland and England and the precise manner of electing the Scottish representatives to the House of Commons and the

House of Lords. These Acts were separately enacted first by the Scottish Parliament (or Estates) and then by the English, which were legislating for their own demise, to be succeeded by the Parliament of Great Britain.

The principal Act was derived, with some slight modifications, from an agreement reached by Commissioners representing each of the two Parliaments, appointed by Queen Anne, who was the monarch of both countries. There was a long history of proposals for union between the countries and attempts made to implement them, in which might be included arranged marriages, the 'Rough Wooing' of Henry VIII, and Cromwell's unification (Ferguson 1977; Levack 1987). But from the beginning of the dual monarchy in 1603 Kings and Queens, faced with the awkwardness of separate Parliaments and institutions in their two realms, had every reason to encourage a political union. Union projects were initiated in 1604, 1640, 1670 and 1702, and although these all proved abortive, they influenced the outcome of the successful project of 1706, when agreement was reached relatively easily, with the whole endeavour completed in nine weeks.

Critics of the Union sometimes observe that the Scottish people did not agree to it. Neither, of course, did the English. Universal adult suffrage was still some two hundred years away, and in the early eighteenth century representative democracy was very imperfectly realised. Daniel Defoe, who was sent to Edinburgh as a government agent in 1706, later wrote in his *History of the Union of Great Britain* (1709) that the Scottish people were 'generally very desirous of the Union' until pamphlets attacking it were circulated. As the terms of the Union became known, some sections of the populace, such as the Jacobites, were more easily stirred to disaffection, and there were riots in Edinburgh and Glasgow.

But in the Scottish Parliament, after clause-by-clause debate, the division on the ratification of the treaty was carried by 110 votes to 69. David Daiches (1977: ch 10) concluded that there was no outright bribery to secure the result, although its likelihood was enhanced by a successful exercise in political jobbery. That is a plausible judgement, because the Crown was not entirely inept in the black arts of political 'management'. But the Crown had not been very successful either. The failures and difficulties in the 'management' of Scotland after 1688 had made it virtually ungovernable (Riley 1974, 1978), which at one and the same time suggests another motive for union and suggests the insufficiency of venality as an explanation for the majority vote.

Perhaps the best distillation of the Scottish parliamentarians' motives is still the summary which was offered on 28 November 1705 by the Earl of Roxburgh to Jerviswood, his ally in the Squadrone Volante group (whose support for the Union, when added to the Court Party's votes, was decisive): 'Trade with most, Hanover with some, ease and security with others, together with a generall aversion at civil discords, intollerable poverty, and the constant oppression of a bad Ministry' (*Baillie of Jerviswood Correspondence*). The chief English motive was security, which would be better ensured if a Hanoverian succession to the throne were accepted throughout Britain. In Scotland motives were mixed, but as the historian Hume Brown (1914: 126) observed, 'it is difficult to escape the conclusion that the men who were chiefly responsible for carrying the Treaty ... were sincerely convinced that union was the only possible solution of the relations between the two kingdoms' (see also Smout 1963, 1969).

The Commissioners on both sides made concessions, and the provisions of the Union legislation are not such as to suggest a shotgun marriage. The position of Scotland's established church had, for example, been kept outside the Commissioners' remit, as being non-negotiable. The English Commissioners were obliged not only to concede freedom of trade and navigation but to grant tax exemptions and payments in compensation. The Scottish Commissioners had to agree to the Hanoverian succession and had to settle for an 'incorporating' union rather than a federal arrangement, a notion which might have been more attractive to some members of the Estates, although there were few models for it and conceptions must have been vague.

The Scottish Commissioners' proposals concerning the legal system and the courts, the royal burghs, and the heritable jurisdictions, engendered no difficulties. As a recent scholar pronounces: 'The men who negotiated the Treaty had no interest in creating a united British nation and therefore enabled the Scots to preserve their own national identity within the Union' (Levack 1987: 212).

Thus some of the institutions and symbols of Scottish nationhood were left untouched by the Union legislation, and in its terms an implication of continuing national identity may be discerned. Even today, if a Westminster Parliament were ever to contemplate, let us say, the abolition of the Scottish courts or the disestablishment of the Church of Scotland, it is arguable that moral or political considerations should dissuade them. It is, however, a different matter to consider whether there is any *legal* impediment to altering or repealing provisions of the Union legislation.

The Union Legislation

Some lawyers have argued that the Union legislation enjoys a special status, so that the UK Parliament is unable to alter some of its more important terms (see Smith 1957; 1962: 49-60; 1987: paras 338-60; Mitchell 1968: ch 4; MacCormick 1978; Upton 1989). The argument is difficult to sustain in the face of the evidence, but it merits some consideration.

Those who argue that Parliament was, in the late Professor Mitchell's memorable phrase 'born unfree', support their case in two ways. Their first point derives from the special nature of the legislation in question. The legislation embodied the terms of a bargain or treaty between representatives of two nations. Moreover, it is found not in an Act, but in *Acts* of Union, and these were enacted by the Scottish and English Parliaments which were effectively signing their own death warrants, not by the Parliament of Great Britain. So the Acts of Union were not only antecedent to the Great Britain Parliament, but may be regarded as constituent: they brought into being a new state, and with it a new Parliament. The proposition is that the legislation may be regarded as a 'fundamental written constitution' (Smith 1961: 207) or a 'constitutional act, which created and limited a Parliament' (Mitchell 1956: 296).

A second and connected argument points to the language of the Union legislation. That the legislation was antecedent to the Parliaments indicates a theoretical possibility that they might be bound by it. That it was intended that succeeding Parliaments should be so restricted is suggested by the wording of the Acts, in which a number of provisions are expressed to be 'fundamental', or to govern 'for ever' or something similar. In addition there are some provisions which are transitional and some which envisage their own alteration, so that it has not been claimed that the Acts in their entirety are sacrosanct, but only that some portions are, which are marked out as of particular importance. For example, the union of the two countries was 'for ever after'. The Court of Session and Court of Justiciary, Scotland's higher courts, were to remain as they were then constituted 'in all time coming', although 'subject nevertheless to such regulations as shall be made by the Parliament of Great Britain'. While the Parliament of Great Britain might legislate freely upon matters of public rights, it was provided that 'no alteration be made in laws which concern private right except for evident utility of the subjects within Scotland'. The Protestant Religion and Presbyterian Church Act 1707 was to be 'held and observed in all time coming as a fundamental and essential condition of any treaty of union ... without any alteration thereof or derogation thereto in any sort for ever'. Language of this sort seems to leave little room for doubt concerning the intentions of those who framed the legislation, and, in construing legislation, it is the duty of the courts to give effect to the intentions of the legislator.

However, these arguments are not so compelling as they first appear. Even if it is correct that the framers of the Union legislation intended that some parts would be unalterable, this would not ensure the fulfilment of their hopes. Legislation which purports to bind future Parliaments will, according to constitutional orthodoxy, simply be ineffective: 'That Parliaments have more than once intended and endeavoured to pass Acts which should tie the hands of their successors is certain, but the endeavour has always ended in failure' (Dicey 1959: 65). The Acts of Union were grist to Dicey's mill, for they afforded 'the strongest proof of the futility'. His views were to find support in cases such as *Vauxhall Estates v Liverpool Corporation* [1932] 1 KB 733 and *Ellen St Estates v Minister of Health* [1934] 1 KB 590. 'The constitutional position', according to Scrutton LJ in the latter case, was that 'Parliament can alter an Act previously passed'. Similarly, Maugham LJ declared that 'the Legislature cannot, according to our constitution, bind itself as to the form of subsequent legislation'.

A capacity to bind subsequent Parliaments should not, therefore, be too readily inferred from the terminology of the Acts. Besides, the language used, unusual as it may sound to our ears, was not exceptional, measured against other enactments of the times. In 1688 the provisions of the Bill of Rights were declared to 'remaine and be the law of this realme for ever', but that had not prevented the English Parliament from altering the succession to the Crown as there laid down twelve years later in the Act of Settlement. The Act of Settlement purported to regulate the coronation oath for all future Kings and Queens, but this has not prevented its amendment. Phrases similar to those found in the Acts of Union were also, as Professor Mitchell (1968: 70) admitted, 'of common occurrence in the Acts of the Parliament of Scotland', but had been ineffective there. In view of this, there is much to be said for a Scottish writer's view that 'the experienced politicians and lawyers of the two countries who drew up the Articles of Union must have been well aware that both parliaments had attempted in the past without success to bind subsequent parliaments, and that the legislature of the UK would find itself under the same disability' (Middleton 1954: 57). Indeed, the lack of any legal bar to a British Parliament's destruction of the treaty guarantees was a point to which attention had been drawn by pamphleteers in Scotland, when they were campaigning to prevent the members of the Estates from agreeing to the Union (Trevelyan 1932: 272; Marshall 1957: 52).

It remains true that the circumstances of the enactment of the Acts of Union were unique. They differ from subsequent statutes in so far as they were passed by different legislatures which thereupon ceased to exist. It is undeniable that the Acts of Union brought a new state into being, although it may be noted that a number of other Acts have also changed the boundaries of the state by addition or subtraction. It seems but a short step further to say, along with Smith (1957), that 'the British Parliament is the creation of the terms of Union' (111), or, with Mitchell (1956), that the Acts 'created ... a Parliament' (296). However, we might jib at that last step. It is true, of course, that there was no Parliament of Great Britain before 1707, but it is difficult to picture 1707 as a completely fresh start. The Instrument of Government, under which Cromwell took office as Lord Protector in 1653, may readily be regarded as a written constitution, in view of its purpose, comprehensiveness, higher law status, and fundamental provisions (in the sense that the authority of governmental institutions derived from the document) (see Munro 1983; 1987: ch 1). But the Acts of Union did not deal systematically with the institutions of government. Even where Parliament was concerned, many aspects of the institution were *not* regulated by the Acts of Union, and the natural reading of the provisions is that aspects of an existing institution were being changed, not that an institution was being established *de novo*. For example, the Acts of Union were silent concerning privileges and procedures as well as on many aspects of composition. Neither the Lords Spiritual, nor the peers of England, nor even the members representing English constituencies in the Commons, who sat in Parliament in 1708, did so under the authority of the Acts of Union. Sheriff Middleton (1954: 53) justifiably considered that 'it would be far-fetched to say that either in form or in substance a new Parliament came into being at Westminster in 1707'.

Thus, the arguments that Parliament was 'born unfree' are less than compelling. We may say, in any event, that arguments about the special nature of the legislation at most show that limitation of Parliament by it is a theoretical possibility, and reference to the language employed at most reveals the aspirations of those who framed the documents.

There is, however, better evidence than this to hand. The question is whether Parliament is restricted by the Acts of Union. It is surely relevant to inquire whether Parliament has felt able to amend them, or has been inhibited from doing so.

Parliament and the Union legislation

Similar arguments about the limiting capacity of the provisions have been advanced in connection with the Union of Great Britain and Ireland in 1800 (Calvert 1968: ch 1). But, of course, that Union, although it was expressed to 'be in force and have effect for ever' was partially dissolved by legislation in 1922 (or earlier, according to the Irish view). In fact, every Article and section in the Union with Ireland Act 1800 (or the corresponding Act of the Irish Parliament) has been repealed or amended. In the light of this, it is, to say the least, difficult still to regard the 1800 legislation as having a binding character. Indeed, the Royal Commission on the Constitution in 1973 used as evidence of the supremacy of Parliament that 'the creation of the Irish Free State in 1922 was made possible by an ordinary Act of Parliament, despite the declared intention of the Act of Union of 1800 that the union of Great Britain and Ireland should last for ever' (para 56).

The Anglo-Scottish Union legislation is not so obviously in tatters. Certainly the union of the countries, their Crowns, and the Parliaments, is still intact, and the Church of Scotland retains its position as the established church in Scotland. But a closer examination reveals that almost all of the articles and sections of the legislation have been amended or repealed in whole or in part. Not all of these repeals constitute 'breaches' of the legislation, of course. Some of the provisions in the Acts of Union were only transitional in duration. Others have been repealed as spent, such as those concerning the first meeting of the new Parliaments (in Article XXII) and the amount of the Scottish contribution when land tax was being raised (in Article IX). There are a number of provisions in which future legislation by the Parliament of Great Britain was contemplated and authorised, such as with regard to the coinage of the realm (Article XVI) and the Scottish Privy Council (Article XIX), abolished in 1708.

Many parts of the legislation neither authorise nor expressly forbid alteration. For example, Article XII and section 6 provide for sixteen peers of Scotland, elected by the larger total number, to sit in the House of Lords and 45 representatives for Scottish constituencies in the House of Commons. But changes in the electoral law from 1832 onwards have resulted in re-drawn constituencies and a greater number of MPs, while the Peerage Act 1963 provided that all peers of Scotland might thereafter sit in the House of Lords.

There are some matters where no alteration is expressly contemplated, and it is arguable that none was intended. Article XXI provides 'That the rights and privileges of the royal burghs of Scotland as they now are do remain entire after the Union and notwithstanding thereof'; and Article XX required that heritable offices and jurisdictions 'be reserved to the owners thereof as rights of property in the same manner as they are now enjoyed by the laws of Scotland notwithstanding this treaty'. Whether clauses such as these were intended to be susceptible to alteration or to be binding is a matter for interpretation. It is a matter of record, however, that the heritable jurisdictions were abolished in 1748 and that the royal burghs lost their functions in 1975.

Finally, there are those parts of the legislation where the terms employed seem more evidently to point to intended entrenchment. There is Article I: the union of the kingdoms is to be 'for ever after'. Article II provides for a common succession to the monarchy, and the barring of Roman Catholics and persons marrying Catholics is 'for ever'. Article VI requires that 'all parts of the United Kingdom for ever from and after the Union shall have the same allowances, encouragements and drawbacks, and be under the same prohibitions, restrictions and regulations of trade ... '; and Article VII that the excises upon liquors shall be uniform in all parts of the new kingdom 'for ever from and after the Union'. Article XVIII, after authorising the new Parliament to alter matters of public right, lays down that 'no alteration be made in laws which concern private right except for evident utility of the subjects within Scotland'. Article XIX deals with the courts: the Court of Session was to 'remain in all time coming within Scotland as it is now constituted by the laws of that kingdom', but 'subject nevertheless to such regulations for the better administration of justice as shall be made by the Parliament of Great Britain', and the Court of Justiciary similarly; the Court of Admiralty in Scotland was to remain as it was 'until the Parliament of Great Britain shall make such regulations and alterations as shall be judged expedient for the whole United Kingdom so as there be always continued in Scotland a Court of Admiralty ... subject nevertheless to such regulations and alterations as shall be thought proper to be made by the Parliament of Great Britain'. By Article XXIV the Scottish regalia and parliamentary and other records and rolls were to remain in Scotland 'in all time coming'.

The Protestant Religion and Presbyterian Church Act 1707, which was incorporated in the Union legislation by both Parliaments, was declared to be 'a fundamental and essential condition of the ... Union in all times coming', and in that Act it was provided that 'the true Protestant religion and the worship, discipline and government' of the established church were 'to continue without any alteration to the people of this land in all succeeding generations'.

Since some parts of the Acts were clearly not intended to be permanent, those who maintain that Parliament is restricted by the Union legislation confine their claim to some of the matters just mentioned. What portions may be included in the category of 'intended to be binding' is a question upon which authorities may disagree. Not only is it doubtful whether Articles XX and XXI were intended to be unalterable, but some of the Articles where phrases implying permanence are employed are nevertheless far from unambiguous. It is interesting, for example, to consider the clauses concerning the courts in Article XIX. Scots lawyers and judges have tended to regard these as fundamental, and therefore forbidding the abolition of the higher Scottish courts. However, it is certainly a possible interpretation of these clauses that reform, or even abolition, by Parliament is authorised if it is 'for the better administration of justice'.

Even the provisions which seem more obviously intended to be binding have not survived unscathed. Scotland and England are still united, but not in the same form. It was accepted without question in 1800 that the Parliament of

Great Britain could merge the country into a wider union with Ireland, which at the same time altered the name of the state and the design of the national flag as they had been specified in Article I of the Union legislation of 1707. There have been encouragements to trade and industry in particular parts of the country, despite the words of Article VI, and, it might be added, to the considerable benefit of Scotland. There have, of course, been numerous alterations to the law of Scotland in matters of 'private right' since 1707, and only persons of an exceptionally trusting or uncritical nature could regard them all as being of 'evident utility'. The Court of Admiralty, the continuing existence of which, upon my reading of Article XIX, was more clearly ordained than that of the other courts mentioned, was abolished in 1830; its jurisdiction in prize having earlier been transferred to the English Court of Admiralty, its remaining civil jurisdiction was then merged in the Court of Session, and its criminal jurisdiction in the Scottish criminal courts. The Court of Session and the High Court of Justiciary have undergone a number of reorganisations and reforms since the Union. Nor have the provisions concerning the established religion been untouched (Lyall 1980). Within a few years of the Union, the British Parliament legislated for toleration in the Scottish Episcopalians Act 1711 and restored lay patronage in the Church Patronage (Scotland) Act 1711. These measures were regarded in Scotland as violations of the spirit of the Union agreement, and the latter was a violation of its letter as well. A requirement in the 1707 Act that professors and masters in universities, colleges and schools had to subscribe to the Confession of Faith did not survive nineteenth-century liberalism: the tests were modified or abolished by the Universities (Scotland) Act 1853, the Parochial and Burgh Schoolmasters (Scotland) Act 1861, and later enactments.

Subscription of the confession by ministers was required by the 1707 Act in the form laid down in a 1693 Act, but the Churches (Scotland) Act 1905 provided a means of amending the formula, which within a few years was employed. Considerable changes in church organisation and government were made in the Church of Scotland Act 1921.

This adds up to a substantial number of amendments and repeals in supposedly unalterable legislation. It may be that on one or two other occasions Parliament has been influenced against potential changes in the law by arguments relying on the terms of the Union legislation, but it is difficult to set much store by this, measured against the numerous amendments which have been carried through. Attempts to explain away the breaches as having been made with consent are selective and profoundly unconvincing. T B Smith (1953: 515) admitted that 'many changes have been made, even of the most fundamental clauses'.

The Union legislation and the courts

The activities of Parliament with regard to the Acts of Union, according to Sir Ivor Jennings (1959: 169), 'at best ... show what Parliament thought of its own powers'. It may be thought that the crucial question *is* what Parliament is able, or not able, effectively to do. However, another question could be asked, concerning the attitude of the courts. If, as some would have us believe, the Acts of Union are to be regarded as a constitutional document which imposes limitations, we should expect to find evidence of this in judicial decisions, and perhaps even a power of judicial review by which enactments contrary to their terms may be declared void.

In reality, there is no instance of legislation being held invalid as being contrary to the Acts of Union; no court in the UK has ever claimed that it could exercise such a power; and on some occasions courts have expressly denied that such a power exists under our constitution.

Certainly, no English court has ever attributed any exceptional effect to the Union legislation. When, in *Ex parte Canon Selwyn* (1872) 36 JP 54, a clergyman attempted to question the validity of the Irish Church Act 1869 (which disestablished the Anglican church in Ireland, contrary to Article 5 of the 1800 Union legislation despite the latter's provision that it was to 'remain in full force for ever'), the Court of Queen's Bench, in dismissing his action, stated that 'there is no judicial body in the country by which the validity of an Act of Parliament' could be questioned, without adding any reservation.

However, it is fair to say that Scottish courts have been less unequivocal. There are dicta in *MacCormick v Lord Advocate* 1953 SC 396 and a few later cases, which give some support to the proposition that the Acts of Union of 1707 are, to some degree and in some sense, 'fundamental law', although the implications of the view are unclear. In fact, it might be more accurate to say that the proposition has been inspired by some unexpected remarks from judges in the 1953 case. It is instructive to notice that a Scottish writer on constitutional law, in his textbook which was in use at that time, quite happily assented to the Diceyan view that Parliament was unlimited (Fraser 1948: 12 ff).

The case of *MacCormick v Lord Advocate* arose from the designation of the present Queen, who had just succeeded to the throne upon her father's death, as 'Elizabeth the Second'. The choice of numeral caused offence to some Scots of nationalist sympathies, for Elizabeth the First had been Queen of England only, and so the designation adopted was questionable. One difficulty for the petitioners was that the Royal Titles Act 1953 empowered Her Majesty to adopt such style and titles as she thought fit. However, it was part of their argument that, since a new state had come into existence in 1707, the enumeration of sovereigns should have begun afresh then; that some of the provisions of the 1707 Acts were fundamental and unalterable, including Article I, which created the state of Great Britain; and that the designation proposed was in conflict with Article I, and should therefore be held illegal.

The Lord Ordinary (Guthrie) who first heard the case found the petitioners' propositions to be 'unsound and indeed extravagant'. On appeal, three judges in the First Division reached the same result. They agreed with the Lord Ordinary that the petition was irrelevant, since nothing in the Acts of Union dealt with royal numerals. They also agreed that the petitioners lacked title to sue. These decisions were sufficient to dispose of the case, but the Lord President, Lord Cooper, added some *obiter dicta* (with which Lord Carmont and Lord Russell expressed agreement):

The principle of the unlimited sovereignty of Parliament is a distinctively English principle which has no counterpart in Scottish constitutional law. It derives its origin from Coke and Blackstone, and was widely popularised during the nineteenth century by Bagehot and Dicey ... Considering that the Union legislation extinguished the Parliaments of Scotland and England and replaced them by a new Parliament, I have difficulty in seeing why it should have been supposed that the new Parliament of Great Britain must inherit all the peculiar characteristics of the English Parliament but none of the Scottish Parliament, as if all that happened in 1707 was that Scottish representatives were admitted to the Parliament of England. That is not what was done. Further the Treaty and associated legislation by which the Parliament of Great Britain was brought into being ... contain some clauses which expressly reserve ... powers of subsequent modification, and other clauses which either contain no such power or emphatically exclude subsequent alteration by declarations that the provision shall be fundamental and unalterable in all time coming, or declarations of a like effect. I have never been able to understand how it is possible to reconcile with elementary canons of construction the adoption by the English constitutional theorists of the same attitude to those markedly different provisions.

These remarks are interesting, although their persuasive force is weakened in several ways.[1] Lord Cooper himself continued in this way:

But the petitioners have still a grave difficulty to overcome on this branch of their argument. Accepting it that there are provisions in the Treaty of Union and associated legislation which are 'fundamental law', and assuming for the moment that something is alleged to have been done – it matters not whether with legislative authority or not – in breach of that fundamental law, the question remains whether such a question is determinable as a justiciable issue in the Courts of either Scotland or England, in the same fashion as an issue of constitutional *vires* would be cognisable by the Supreme Courts of the United States, or of South Africa or Australia. I reserve my opinion with regard to the provisions relating expressly to this Court and to the laws 'which concern private right' which are administered here. This is not such a question, but a matter of 'public right' ... This at least is plain, that there is neither precedent nor authority of any kind for the view that the domestic Courts of either Scotland or England have jurisdiction to determine whether a governmental act of the type here in controversy is or is not conform to the provisions of a Treaty, least of all when that Treaty is one under which both Scotland and England ceased to be independent states and merged their identity in an incorporating union.

Sir Thomas Smith (1961: 209) drew from Lord Cooper's judgment the implication that 'legislation may be illegal and unconstitutional without necessarily being subjected to scrutiny and restraint by the judiciary'. On this view, the matter of fundamental status is one question, and the matter of justiciability is another. Certainly, such a distinction may be drawn (see Walker and Himsworth 1991), but if the focus is on practical consequences, we should remember Lord Cooper's own appreciation that 'it is of little avail to ask whether the Parliament of Great Britain 'can' do this thing or that, without going on to inquire who can stop them if they do' (1953 SC at 412).

Dicta in several subsequent Scottish cases have been equally Janus-like. Typically these judicial observations have concealed more than they revealed. Sometimes there has been acceptance of the view that a few provisions in the Union legislation may be regarded as in some way 'fundamental', but it has been combined with a denial of justiciability or an avoidance of the issue. Thus, in *Gibson v Lord Advocate* 1975 SC 136, while the Lord Ordinary (Lord Keith) in *obiter dicta* preferred to reserve his opinion on the effect of (hypothetical) Acts purporting to abolish the Court of Session or the Scottish legal system or the Church of Scotland, he considered that arguments about whether alterations in private law were 'for the evident utility' of the subjects within Scotland would *not* be justiciable, and upheld the validity of EC fishery laws (imported via the European Communities Act 1972) as being in the realm of public law which Parliament was free to alter. In *Sillars v Smith* 1982 SLT 539, the High Court of Justiciary was faced with an argument that Parliament's authority to legislate had been lost when it failed to bring into force the devolution provisions of the Scotland Act 1978 following the referendum in 1979. The court bluntly dismissed the contention, citing with approval Lord Cooper's *disclaimer* of jurisdiction to question Acts of Parliament in *MacCormick v Lord Advocate* and the declaration of Lord Campbell in the House of Lords in a nineteenth-century appeal from the Court of Session that 'All that a court of justice can do is look to the Parliament Roll' (*Edinburgh and Dalkeith Rly Co v Wauchope* (1842) 8 Cl + Fin 710, 725). More recently, a group of cases involved challenges to the community charge (or 'poll tax') legislation, notoriously introduced in Scotland a year earlier than in England and Wales. Some of them did not proceed beyond the Sheriff Court, but three of them reached the Inner House of the Court of Session. In *Pringle, Petitioner* 1991 SLT 330, there was an attempt to invoke the *nobile officium* of the court to obtain relief, on the argument that the earlier imposition of the community charge in Scotland was contrary to Article IV, which provided for equal advantages. The Inner House held that the jurisdiction could not be invoked to override express provisions of statute law, with the Lord President and Lord Weir reserving their opinion on whether a breach of Article IV was involved in such circumstances.

In *Murray v Rogers* 1992 SLT 221 and *Fraser v MacCorquodale* 1992 SLT 229, defaulting residents argued that the Abolition of Domestic Rates etc (Scotland) Act 1987 was contrary to Article XVIII, but the appeals were rejected for incompetence, it being held impossible to challenge the validity of the Act under the statutory jurisdiction created by that very Act, as the appellants were seeking to do. An argument that doubts over the validity of the Act might constitute a 'reasonable excuse' for failure to register timeously was also rejected as unsustainable. Besides, in *Fraser* the Lord President considered it 'questionable whether the issues which the applicant seeks to raise are justiciable in any court', and in *Murray*, Lord Kirkwood stated more unequivocally that 'there is, so far as I am aware, no machinery whereby the validity of an Act of Parliament can be brought under review by the courts'.

Lord Kirkwood's frankness is welcome. Some other Scottish judges have indulged in some huffing and puffing before, like the wolf, slinking away. But the realities are clear enough. When a Royal Commission on the Constitution was set up in response to demands in the 1960s for greater devolution of power to Scotland and Wales, independence or separatism was one of the possibilities considered by it under its terms of reference. The government obviously thought that legislation to that effect was perfectly possible. So did the Royal Commission, which in its later stages was chaired by the Scottish judge, Lord Kilbrandon. 'The supremacy of Parliament', they said, 'has the consequence that it is not bound by the acts of its predecessors ... No special procedures are required to enact even the most fundamental changes in the constitution' (para 56).

Scotland in the Union

In the previous section, it was demonstrated that there is no legal impediment to alteration of the Acts of Union. Persistent claims to the contrary rendered the demonstration necessary. But there is an air of unreality about the controversy since, as already observed, numerous alterations have in fact occurred.

Many repeals and amendments have been made because specific economic and political arrangements which were thought appropriate in 1707 were seen as inappropriate or unnecessary at a later date. Some provisions simply became spent with the passage of time. Thus items relating to ship registration, customs and excise duties for specified goods, the Equivalents (transfers of money agreed in the terms), the Scottish mint, weights and measures, the Court of Exchequer, Privy Council and parliamentary elections became otiose or were superseded, and Statute Law Revision Acts of 1867, 1871, 1906 and 1948 repealed nine Articles wholly and five others in part.

Incidentally, many of the reforms effected were obviously beneficial. It could not seriously be argued that the corrupt electoral system which existed before the 1832 Reform Act should have been maintained, or that the heritable jurisdictions, which were the main prop of feudal society in rural Scotland, should have been preserved. And had not the Act securing the Protestant Religion been amended, then the appointment of university professors would still be subject to a religious test.

Thus it may be seen that there is ample precedent for alterations when changing conditions justify them. Some scholars and sometimes politicians have displayed an obsession with the precise terms of the 1707 legislation (and possible alterations or more pejoratively 'breaches' of it). But it is an unhealthy obsession. Those who suffer from the neurosis fail to appreciate the extent to which the evolution of society since 1707 has been reflected in evolution of the Union notwithstanding the precise terms of the provisions as they were enacted then.

The larger question to which we should turn is the success or failure of the endeavour to retain three separate nations in a political union (Wales having been joined to England earlier, but by conquest rather than union) as Great Britain, or four as the UK.

It is instructive to notice that we do regard Scotland and Wales, for example, as *nations*, and not merely as regions of a unitary state. If the unions which created the UK had been intended to produce a complete assimilation, and if the intention had succeeded, then the identities of the constituent nations would have been swallowed up in a UK or 'British' identity, and Scots would merely be 'North Britons'. Some persons may even have hoped that such an assimilation would occur, although the terms of the Union legislation in 1707 would suggest that assimilation was not intended.

In any event, what may be declared with confidence is that assimilation has not occurred. Elements of distinctive traditions, characteristics and culture have survived in Scotland and in other parts of the UK, and contribute to feelings of separate national identity. Indeed, opinion polls would suggest that most persons residing in Scotland primarily feel that they are Scottish. But is is perhaps truer to say that the people of Scotland feel themselves to be Scottish and British, for the identities are not incompatible. It may even be argued that the enduring achievement of the treaty in 1707 has been the preservation of national sentiments within an over-arching union.

Continuing distinctiveness of the nations in cultural and other aspects would not necessarily be reflected in constitutional arrangements. It is conceivable that the UK, as a sovereign state, might have a single legislature, a single executive government, and a single legal system, without any differentiation of arrangements for the constituent nations. But such is not the case. There are constitutional features which are different in respect of the nations which comprise the UK. Therefore, it may be said that there is constitutional recognition of the nationhood of Scotland within the framework of union. This recognition is afforded in ways that do not apply to, for example, the (more populous) North-West of England. In order properly to describe Scotland in the Union, we should remind ourselves what these distinctive features are, and what they amount to. They may be considered under four headings: the Scottish legal system; Scotland in Parliament; administrative devolution; and civil society.

The Scottish legal system

When reviewing the Scottish dimension in legislative and executive matters, the question is to what extent there are differences of treatment, so that there are special arrangements either in addition to, or in partial substitution of, UK-wide arrangements.

But in considering the third branch of government, the situation differs because there is not a UK or 'British' legal system. The sovereign state of the UK comprises three legal systems.

Scots law was markedly different from English in 1681, when Viscount Stair published his *Institutions*, representing it as a coherent system of principles fashioned from various sources, but principally native custom, case law, feudal law, Roman law, Canon law and the law of nature. The Institutional Writers themselves provided a source of Scots law which had no English counterpart. The High Court of Justiciary, dating from the twelfth century, had become Scotland's principal criminal court, and in 1532 the Court of Session had been established in Edinburgh as the leading civil court.

Provisions in the Union legislation of 1707 were designed to ensure that the law of Scotland would remain distinct and that the separate Scottish court system would be preserved. In principle, these aims have been fulfilled. There have been judicature reforms, especially by Acts of 1747, 1808, 1810, 1830, 1856, 1887, 1926, 1975 and 1988, and the High Court and Court of Session, as reconstituted, have common personnel, but they remain in being as courts of criminal and civil jurisdiction respectively, and the High Court of Justiciary in its appellate capacity is at the apex of the criminal court hierarchy. In matters of civil law, the House of Lords became recognised after 1707 as the highest court of appeal. Although the House sits as an appellate court for Scots law, or English, or Northern Irish, as the case may be, the similarity between the systems has tended gradually to increase under its influence, and through the actions of a common legislature in Parliament which, although it may legislate for or omit to legislate for any one of the three systems, may also legislate for all three or for two of them. Membership of the EU has, of course, also led to unification or harmonisation of laws in the systems, in areas of Community competence. Nonetheless, while there are fields of Scots law (such as company law or social security law) which are nearly identical to English law, there are other fields (such as land law or criminal procedure) which are substantially different, and the systems remain not only analytically distinct but observably diverse. The distinctness of the Scottish legal system allows the law on a variety of matters to differ from England's and often requires the enactment of separate legislation, even when the same end is in view.

Scotland in Parliament

Scotland's representation in the House of Commons is generous, as is Wales's. There is a 'Celtic preference' inherent in the rules concerning parliamentary constituencies, which are found in the Parliamentary Constituencies Act 1986. Instead of providing (as it might) that all constituencies should consist of equal numbers of electors, the legislation prescribes minimum numbers of constituencies for Scotland, Wales and Northern Ireland (but not for England) within the total, and establishes four Boundary Commissions to review and report for their respective national territories.

Under the legislation, Scotland must have no fewer than 71 constituencies (and it does in fact currently have 72). In 1991 the average size of electorate in Scottish constituencies was 54,369, and the average size in England was 69,279. It has been calculated that if arithmetical equality throughout the UK were the basis, then Scotland's entitlement would be to 58 or 59 seats instead of 72. Thus, the 'Celtic preference' is quite significant, and it is realistic to view it as a concession to Scottish nationhood within the Union. It is also salutary to recall that, while a Northern Ireland Parliament sat at Stormont under a system of legislative devolution, there was a reduction in representation at Westminster (from 17 seats to 12). Therefore, one may doubt whether Scotland's over-representation at Westminster would survive, if a Scottish Parliament should ever be created without corresponding institutions in England.

As things stand, the UK Parliament is the only legislature. As already observed, it may legislate for the UK in its entirety, or so as to have application only in one (or more) of the constituent parts. As to how Parliament *ought* to act in this regard, there are no hard and fast rules, but there are some rather ill-defined expectations. It would be expected that in most matters of private law and generally in those areas of public affairs which are administered in the Scottish Office, there would be distinct provision for Scotland (which does not necessarily require distinct Acts), but it is fair to say that Scottish expectations have sometimes been disappointed. Shortage of parliamentary time is the root of the problem, but governments have left themselves open to accusations of Anglocentricity, when they have either failed to find sufficient time for distinctive legislation or have been insensitive to different traditions. However, since the publication of the report of the Renton Committee on the Preparation of Legislation in 1975 (Cmd 6053), some of the more obvious manifestations of insensitivity, such as ill-conceived adaptation clauses, have been less evident.

Some variations in the usual parliamentary processes may be made for Bills (or parts of Bills) which are exclusively Scottish in application. The procedural rules of the House of Commons allow for such proposals to be debated by the Scottish Grand Committee (consisting of all 72 Scottish MPs) at the Second Reading stage instead of in the House itself, if fewer than ten members object. For the committee stage, where matters of detail are debated and resolved, Scottish Bills are sent to one of two Scottish Standing Committees, composed of upwards of sixteen members, mostly Scottish. Since 1980, the Scottish Grand Committee has been able to meet in Scotland, and in 1993 the Government published proposals for enhancing its role, with more frequent meetings, more debates, and Question Time sessions being envisaged (Scottish Office 1993). Even if these special arrangements for parliamentary business affecting Scotland were only symbolic, they would signify some recognition of nationhood. But they amount to rather more than that. They constitute a Scottish parliamentary sub-system which, if properly utilised, enables Scottish business to be differently handled.

Administrative devolution

The UK does exhibit what may be called administrative devolution, where the central government, without creating assemblies or executive governments in different regions or parts, arranges for aspects of its work to be conducted by a department which is defined *territorially* rather than *functionally*. Scotland, Wales, and (in rather different circumstances) Northern Ireland are favoured in this way.

After the Union in 1707, there was no reason of principle why special arrangements should be made for Scotland in the matter of executive government. Yet in the eighteenth century political management made of Scotland virtually a separate satrapy, and in the nineteenth government functions were often carried out separately through agencies such as the Fisheries Board and the Prison Board. Then in 1885, at a time when the Irish home rule question had become pressing, it was decided to differentiate the handling of Scottish affairs more clearly. So a Scottish Office was created as a department of government, whose minister, the Secretary for Scotland, was to be responsible for law and order, education, and a few other matters. From 1892, it became the practice to allocate a place in the Cabinet to the minister, and in 1926 his office was raised in status to that of a Secretary of State. Since 1939, the principal base of the Scottish Office has been in Edinburgh.

Over the years, the functions and importance of the Scottish Office have gradually been increased. Today the Secretary of State, with four junior ministers, and a Scottish Office organised in five departments, is responsible for agriculture and fisheries, the arts, crofting, education, the environment, the fire service, forestry, health, housing, industrial assistance, some legal matters (with other functions falling to the Lord Advocate's Department), local government, police, prisons, roads, rural and urban development, social work, sport, transport, tourism and town planning, as well as some minor departments and public corporations, in so far as they operate in Scotland. In some other matters the minister is jointly responsible with another minister (who has the relevant functional responsibility). More generally, as one committee put it, 'there is a wide and undefined area in which he is expected to be the mouthpiece of Scottish opinion in the Cabinet and elsewhere' (Scottish Office 1937: para 37).

The Secretary of State system is something of an untidy compromise, for extensive powers of government are not properly matched by a corresponding political base. The 'territorial' Secretaries of State may have the appearance of being colonial governors, especially when their political affiliation differs from the majority of the territory's MPs.

Nevertheless, the system also has considerable merits. Scotland, in acknowledgment of its nationhood, receives some special consideration which is denied to regions of England, and there can be little doubt that it has profited. Certainly, it has enjoyed a higher expenditure per head of population than other parts of Great Britain, and it is reasonable to attribute this in part to the advantage of having a spokesman of Cabinet rank. Administration has probably been better by reason of the Scottish Office civil servants being closer to the country's concerns and its people. Policies which apply to the whole kingdom may be applied with Scottish conditions in mind. Policies formulated in areas such as social work and education, where there are differences, have often compared favourably with the English equivalents.

Civil society

Administrative devolution may be regarded as a kind of 'regional' government. At the lower level, local government has always been differently organised in Scotland. The royal burghs were left intact in 1707, but in its modern form local government is the product of the expansion of public activity in the nineteenth century. There were major reforms in 1889, 1929 and 1975, and another is in contemplation.

Legislative, executive and judicial arrangements are indisputably part of government, in its broader sense, but there is another dimension which we may call civil society, comprising those institutions and phenomena which operate in the public domain or are part of national culture but are not part of government. In this realm too, Scotland is different.

Religion may be included as part of civil society, although the 'establishment' of churches which exists in Scotland and in England (but neither in Wales nor in Northern Ireland) signifies some connection to the state. In Scotland, especially following controversies and schisms in the nineteenth century, the bonds are loose, indeed almost non-existent. Scotland has a different established church, the protestant Church of Scotland with its presbyterian government. The established Church of England, formed by King Henry VIII after the Pope declined to annul his first marriage, is episcopal and closer to Roman Catholicism in doctrine, and there the nexus of church and state (with its drawbacks as well as its privileges) is much stronger. As a totem of Scottish nationhood, the church (or Kirk) figures prominently in the Union legislation, and ever since its influence on Scottish society, in politics and morals as well as in religious affairs, has been very considerable, even if today it is waning. Religion still marks Scotland out, with a higher proportion of Roman Catholics in the population than England as well as a different majority protestant denomination, and rather different attitudes and influences.

Along with law and religion, education is traditionally viewed as another totem of Scottish distinctiveness. Amongst the differences taken to characterise the Scottish approach are greater openness and accessibility of educational provision for all, regardless of background, broadly-based curricula and examination systems, a combination of three-year Ordinary and four-year Honours degree courses in universities, and higher participation rates in higher education than in England and Wales. A different heritage and different traditions have contributed to these characteristics. In recent times, although not uninfluenced by developments in England and elsewhere, Scotland has continued to go its own way. Indeed, the differentiation has increased in some respects (for example, with Scottish universities put under a separate funding council since 1992).

There are other aspects of civil society in which Scotland is quite distinguishable. For example, there are different organs of the media, with differences in content and in tone. There are different architectural traditions, and different patterns of domestic housing. There are differences in Scottish industry and trade, and in agriculture and fisheries, which is not to deny that the wealth of the Scottish economy is dependent on conditions elsewhere.

In a host of ways, Scotland is different. Some of these contrasts were in mind in 1707, when some thought was given to maintaining them, and the separateness of the legal system perhaps owes something to the moral force of these considerations. There are other matters, such as religion and local government, where provisions of 1707 have not been allowed to stand in the way of change, and there are spheres such as education where a distinctive Scottishness owes nothing to the Union legislation as such. Indeed, some of the allowances for Scotland in parliamentary arrangements and executive government were not at all in contemplation in 1707.

Alternatives

Scotland, in acknowledgment of its nationhood, receives special treatment, but the UK remains a unitary state, with a supreme Parliament and a single executive government. As a compromise, it has merits. But it may not be what everyone wants. In this concluding section, we briefly consider some of the alternatives. First, to dispose of a couple of *canards*.

Recalling the Scottish Parliament

Some campaigners and some politicians have advocated the recall of the Scottish Parliament. The demand may have some purchase as an appeal to emotions, but it would seem to have little grounding in reality. There is, of course, no Scottish Parliament to recall. It is an interesting curiosity, which may have emboldened these campaigners, that the Acts of Union did not in terms abolish the Scottish Parliament (or, for that matter, the English). Besides, it was sometimes believed that the Parliament was merely adjourned on 25 March 1707 when it met for the last time and the Lord Chancellor, Seafield, remarked on the 'end of an auld sang'. In fact, as the historian Ferguson notes, the Parliament was not merely adjourned but was dissolved by proclamation on 28 April 1707, as Privy Council records show (Ferguson 1977: 266).

Whether there was adjournment or dissolution scarcely matters, since the Parliament, having had no effective operation since 1707, has no legal existence either (see JTC 1961). Its mixture of Scottish nobility, barons of the shires and burgesses, along with up to eight nominees of the Crown as Officers of State, could hardly be reconstituted, given that neither the royal burghs (since 1975) nor the electoral areas exist as such any more. We may also think it unlikely that the Sovereign will be minded to use her prerogative to summon such an assembly and, as Rait (1924: 315) says concerning the Scottish Parliament, 'the necessity of a royal summons was universally admitted'. In short, the suggestion of 'recall' is anachronistic and merely fanciful.

Re-negotiation of the Union

Another demand which features in the political rhetoric is for 're-negotiation' of the Union. Immediately, we are confronted by a paradox. Since the suggestion often emanates from those of a nationalist persuasion or persons who are hostile to the Union, there seems to be some confusion of purpose or at least language. Perhaps what these persons are seeking, in coded terms, is independence (or disunion). There would, of course, have to be some political processes to achieve that result (as with the recognition of the Irish Free State in 1922) and there would no doubt be foreign relations to be pursued afterwards, by negotiation or otherwise. But to call these processes a 're-negotiation of the Union' would seem to be a misdescription. Besides, we may observe an inconsistency in so far as the same persons claim at the same time that the terms of the 1707 Union are unalterable and that there should be re-negotiation to alter them.

In fact, as we have seen, there have been numerous alterations already, many of them to Scotland's advantage. There has been a continuing process of re-negotiation, as Scottish members and English members and others in the UK Parliament have found it appropriate to repeal or amend provisions of the Union legislation. Of course, some persons who have called for re-negotiation may consider that the advantages and recognition which Scotland enjoys amount to less than Scotland deserves, while accepting that Scotland should remain part of the UK. Such a view would at least be coherent, whether it is justified being another question. But there are obvious practical difficulties attaching to any 're-negotiation', of which the problem of deciding how 'Scotland' and 'England' should be represented in one would merely be the first.

More serious proposals for a change in constitutional arrangements, if they are not calls for independence, generally involve a demand for a Scottish Parliament either as part of a federal system or as a further measure of 'devolution'. There is not space here for a full discussion of these issues, but a few remarks may be offered about these alternatives.

Independence

The other essays in this collection are concerned with different aspects of the implications of independence as against the circumstances of continuing union.

As is demonstrated by the example of the Republic of Ireland, political events may lead to a separation within the UK. In such an eventuality, there would be no merely *legal* impediment to Scotland's becoming independent (although there would be many legal and other complications to be resolved, if it were ever to happen).

Irish independence came about after a general election when Sinn Fein, the revolutionary independence movement, won 124 out of the 128 seats outside the six counties which were to compose 'Northern Ireland', and the elected representatives did not take their places at Westminster. The Scottish National Party reached the height of its popularity with 11 seats at the October 1974 general election, but in 1987 and again in 1992 won only 3 seats out of Scotland's 72.

Federalism

'Federalism' is a term sometimes used loosely but, as classically defined, it involves 'a division of powers between general and regional authorities, each of which, in its own sphere, is co-ordinate with the others and independent of them' (Wheare 1963: 33). With the United States of America as a model, the federal principle has attracted interest and some admiration, since the eighteenth century.

But admiration has not been universal or unqualified. Dicey (1967: 171, 173, 175), preferring the legislative supremacy of the UK Parliament, summed up unfavourably: 'Federal government means weak government ... Federalism tends to produce conservatism ... Federalism, lastly, means legalism'. Sir Ivor Jennings (1953: 55), who did not very often agree with Dicey, remarked that 'nobody would have a federal constitution if he could possibly avoid it', and Harold Laski (1939) predicted the disappearance of the phenomenon. Even supporters of the federal principle emphasise that federalism is not an easy option. By definition, it necessitates more complex constitutional arrangements than a unitary state, and it demands sufficient economic resources to support two independent levels of government. Only a minority of states in the world, numbering fewer than thirty, may be classified as federal today.

Many of the federal states of the world, such as Australia, Canada and India, occupy large territories, so that geographical factors appear to be relevant. It is also interesting to note that federations have much more often resulted from a 'bargain' to *form* a state than from a process of fission within an existing unitary state.

Dicey (1967: 142) asserted that 'the experience of England and Scotland in the eighteenth century shows that the sense of common interests, or common national feeling, may be too strong to allow of that combination of union and separation which is the foundation of federalism'. That assertion may be rather too bland for some tastes, but there is not much comfort for advocates of a federal UK in the studies by political scientists of the factors favourable to the creation, operation, and continuation of federations (which, we should notice, are three different questions). Some of the prerequisites suggested by Wheare (1963: ch 3) (such as previous political association, naturally, and similarity of political institutions) could be said to exist, but others (such as a sense of military insecurity, and a divergence of economic interests) are not obviously present. William Riker (1964) suggested that security against common enemies was the central motive behind all federations. Thomas Franck (1968), on the basis of a study of failed federations, considered the essential condition for success to be 'a commitment to the primary ideal of federalism'.

If it may be doubted whether the circumstances are favourable in a general way, there are additionally reasons to believe that one possible pattern, a federation of the four historic nations of the UK, would not be satisfactory. Geoffrey Sawer (1976: 108), who refined Wheare's list of prerequisites, added others including 'a sufficient number of federating units (probably at least five) to prevent continuous face to face conflict of one or two potential region rivals' and 'a relationship of size/resources/population between units such that no one or combination of two can dominate a combination of the rest'. History provides examples of federations which, lacking these conditions, did not succeed, like the Rhodesian Federation and Nigeria.

Other patterns would be possible, if England (at least) were divided into several regions for the purpose of establishing a federal UK. However, there is an absence of regional identity in England or at least parts of England, so that such an exercise would be artificial and problematic, which is not to say that it could not be done. The Royal Commission on the Constitution considered that 'there is very little demand for federalism in Scotland and Wales, and practically none at all in England', and it concluded that there were 'general objections to federalism as a form of government' as well as 'considerations which would make it particularly unsuitable for adoption in the United Kingdom' (paras 498, 525). The Commission was perhaps too briskly dismissive of a principle which has its uses, but it is fair to say that, as things stand, there is nothing approaching a consensus on either the merits or the practicalities of applying the federal principle to the UK.

Devolution

'Devolution' is an even more imprecise term than federalism, but generally connotes the dispersal of power from a superior to an inferior political authority. There are measures of administrative devolution within the UK, as we have seen. But when critics of the *status quo* in Scotland speak of devolution, it is shorthand for legislative devolution. They want a Scottish Parliament.

Under a comprehensive scheme of legislative devolution, the UK Parliament would remain as supreme, but Parliaments would be established in the nations and regions of the state to deal with such matters as were devolved to them. But some of the same difficulties observed in relation to federalism would apply equally again. Another layer of government would be added, which would have to be paid for. The responsibilities and relations of the central and the regional bodies would have to be delineated. It would have to be decided whether the regional Parliaments would have tax-raising powers, with the consequences entailed in that, or would be dependent on central grants (which might be deleterious to them or might be a continuing cause of friction). Unsatisfactory financial arrangements are thought to have contributed to the failure of the Stormont Parliament system (Calvert 1970). Again, we should notice that there is little or no demand for an English Parliament or for Parliaments in the English regions. Some of these difficulties would dissolve or be lessened in so far as the regional assemblies had a more limited role, which is perhaps the most attractive solution in the interests of minimising both costs and potential for divisiveness. Perhaps neither opponents nor proponents of national Parliaments would be satisfied with such an outcome, but this may be an appropriate juncture to remind ourselves that in the 1979 referendums only 11.9% of the electorate in Wales voted in favour of creating an elected assembly with an executive role, and 32.9% of the electorate in Scotland voted in favour of a Scottish Assembly with legislative powers.

Many campaigners in Scotland, perhaps indifferent to what happens elsewhere, seem to confine their demands to the creation of a Scottish Parliament. But a unilateral devolution scheme, if it avoids certain problems (such as the division of England into artificial regions for unwanted purposes), creates others. Notoriously, the 'West Lothian question' arises if a government contemplates devolving power to some portions of the state while otherwise maintaining a unitary Parliament and government. As Mr. Tam Dalyell (1977: 247) put it:

> We would have the absurd situation in which Scottish and Welsh MPs could continue to legislate on subjects which had been devolved to the Assemblies in their own countries. They would not be responsible to their own constituents for such legislation, nor would they be answerable to the English voters who would be affected by it.

The lesson to be drawn is that 'it is impossible to seal off the government of one part of a unitary state from the government of other parts' (Marquand 1989: 392). This perception may have eluded the majority of the Royal Commissioners who reported on the constitution in 1973, but it did not escape the two Commissioners (Professor Alan Peacock and Lord Crowther-Hunt) who wrote a forceful Memorandum of Dissent. These two also noted that an attitude survey had shown almost as much discontent with the existing system in English regions as in Scotland and Wales, and were prompted by considerations of justice to propose a uniform scheme of seven elected assemblies (which would not have had legislative powers). After all, if a Parliament or assembly means better government, then why should Scotland and Wales be given it if Wessex (also once a separate kingdom) and North-West England (more populous than either) are not? Some recognition of ancient nationhood is one thing, but a blueprint for a future constitutional reform is something else. It should be remembered that Labour MPs from the North of England were prominent in the rebellion which killed off the Callaghan government's first devolution bill.

Unilateral devolutionists tend to ignore or minimise these considerations, but they should not be underestimated. Not only are there awkward constitutional problems involved. It is also politically naive to imagine that Her Majesty's Government and the UK Parliament will happily implement schemes which alter arrangements radically for some parts of Great Britain without thought for the other parts, and which, as some of their supporters freely confess, could be steps on a slippery slope leading to independence.

Conclusion

The British constitution is evolving and changing (Munro 1994), perhaps more than is generally realised, but further reforms are certainly desirable. Amongst these, there is a case for decentralisation of government to be carried further, and the case may possibly be strengthened by influences from the EU, which has an as yet rather underdeveloped regional policy. Although the UK is sometimes depicted as a highly centralised state, it incorporates some quasi-federal features (such as by having three legal systems) and it affords recognition of the different nationhood of Scotland, Wales, and Northern Ireland in diverse ways. If the Union has amounted to more than the sum of its parts, as many of us believe, then we should build on that success by considering the potential benefits and the potential costs of possible reforms, rationally and unemotionally, and from a UK perspective. The opposite path may lead to the Balkanisation of Britain, and that way madness lies.

Scottish, English and British Culture

Allan Massie

It is a common, and justified, complaint, that the English, even the educated English, are sadly ignorant of Scotland. If an Englishman was to retort that the Scots – or at any rate the Scottish cultural nationalists, – display a comparable and equally culpable ignorance of England, he would, north of the Border, meet with a scornful and incredulous response. Yet there would be as much truth in his charge as in our complaint.

Our cultural nationalists like to boast of Scotland's links with the Continent, as if a debt to France was a matter of pride, and a debt to England of shame. Much of what they say about our connections with France, the Netherlands, Scandinavia, Germany, and Italy is of course true. The hybrid nature of Scots law, itself such an influential strand in our cultural inheritance, undoubtedly connects us with the European legal tradition in a way that English lawyers are not connected. It is likewise perfectly true to say, as Paul H Scott (1991: 58-59) does, that David Hume 'was as much at home in Paris as in Edinburgh, but he disliked London, and, in his own words, "the barbarians who inhabit the Banks of the Thames"' – in which observation, however, I, unlike Mr Scott, detect a note of humourous flyting. (Nevertheless he wrote a *History of England*, not of France.) It is equally right that Mr Scott should remind us that Dugald Stewart attributed 'the sudden burst of genius' in the Scotland of the Enlightenment to the fact that 'from time immemorial, a continuous intercourse had been kept up between Scotland and the Continent'. It is right to insist on the debt which Scotland owes to Calvin, though, while doing so, it might be prudent to remember that the greatest English poet after Shakespeare, Milton, was similarly indebted. It is correct to acknowledge what our architectural tradition owes to France, but we should not, in doing so, be blind to the influence of Palladio on the English country house. The Scots painters of the eighteenth century all flocked to Rome; but so did most of the English artists; and the lessons they learned were similar.

In short, if we insist on our openness to the cultural influence of France and Italy, while pretending that the country which Sir Walter Scott called 'our sister and ally', was somehow impervious to similar influences we throw ourselves open to charges of absurdity. There was as constant a traffic between England and the Continent as between Scotland and the Continent; and it is impossible to read Chaucer (whom our great poet Dunbar regarded as his master) or Shakespeare (whom Scott quotes more frequently than any other author) without being aware of how deeply both were influenced by French and Italian literature. It would indeed be remarkable if it were not so. To pretend that Scotland is somehow 'more European' than England is an empty boast, evidence of that sense of cultural inferiority against which our cultural nationalists would have us guard ourselves.

Any rich culture is composed of a number of different strains. Half a dozen at least may be identified in ours. There is first the Gaelic or Celtic strain, which may indeed be held to set us apart from English culture, even though Matthew Arnold made a brave attempt to identify what he considered to be the Celtic note in English literature. There is what I shall content myself for the moment with calling the Anglo-Saxon strain, common to almost the whole of England and the south and east of Scotland. There is what again for the moment I shall identify only as the Christian strain, and there is the strain which we have inherited from Antiquity and the cultures of Greece and Rome.

Now of these elements that go to form what may be called Scottish culture, only the first separates us from England, though of course it separates us every bit as completely from Europe. The history of the past thousand years has been the story of the long and gradual retreat of Gaeldom. It began centuries before the Union of the Crowns, as the Celts came under pressure from the Norsemen in the north and west, and from Anglo-Saxon culture in the south and east. Whether the Anglo-Saxon tongue was introduced to Scotland from Northumbria or directly from the Continent by those who created and settled the burghs of lowland Scotland may remain matter for dispute; it is probable that both influences went to form the culture of lowland Scotland. At any rate there is evidence that before the Norman Conquest of England, Anglo-Saxon (or Old English) had become the language of the Lothians. The influence which Queen (later St) Margaret exercised over her husband Malcolm Canmore, who had himself gained his throne from his rival Macbeth only with the help of the Northumbrian earls, determined that Scotland came under the sway of the Catholic Church of Rome, and that the old Celtic Church of the Culdees, which traced its ancestry to St Columba, virtually disappeared. Margaret's youngest son, David I, king of Scots 1124-53, on the one hand took advantage of the weakness of the English monarchy in Stephen's reign to establish the complete independence of Scotland, and in like manner strove to gain independence also for the Church in Scotland by seeking metropolitan status for the see of St Andrews and rejecting the authority claimed by the Archbishop of York; but on the other hand, through his own links with the Anglo-Norman baronage, and by his grants of lands to Anglo-Norman families like the Balliols, Bruces, Comyns and Stewarts, many of whom held estates in England as well as Scotland, bound lowland Scotland within the common feudal culture of Western Europe.

The Wars of Independence may have retarded, but could not check, this process. They certainly fixed a sense of Scottish identity, which had scarcely existed before. They created the basis for a distrust of English ambitions, and for an animosity to England which has never quite died away. They led to the formation of the 'Auld Alliance' with France, of which both countries retain an agreeable and sentimental memory. In time they produced our first two nationalist poems, Barbour's 'Brus' and Blind Harry's 'Wallace', both of which were however written in the northern version of the English language.

A word on that language is necessary here, if only because patriotic obfuscation over the centuries has successfully obscured the relationship between Scots and English.

Scots, it may be said, is neither a dialect of English, nor a distinct language. It cannot be the latter because there is virtually no grammatical distinction to be made between any variety of Scots and standard English. It cannot be called a dialect, which Chambers' Dictionary defines as 'a variety or form of a language peculiar to a district or class, especially but not necessarily other than a literary or standard form', unless Chaucerian English is to be called that also.

The matter is best approached historically. Philologists distinguish three varieties of Old English: the South-western, Midland, and Northern. The first did indeed dwindle into a dialect, represented in modern literature by some of the dialogue in Hardy's novels and by the poetry of William Barnes. The Midlands variety, being the language spoken from about 1400 at the English Court, in London, and at the universities of Oxford and Cambridge, developed in time into what is now recognized as Standard English. The history of the Northern variety is more complicated. Very briefly, though originally the tongue spoken from the Humber to Aberdeen, it divaricated owing to the influence of the political boundary eventually fixed between England and Scotland. South of that Border it lacked the stimulus necessary for the full development of a language and eventually dwindled to the point where it appeared a mere variant of Standard English confined to a narrow and principally rustic use.

Its history in Scotland was different, for being there the tongue of the royal court and aristocracy, it became the language used in law and administration, the language of a high rather than merely rustic culture. By the fifteenth century, though still known to even its literary users as 'Inglis', it had become a rich and versatile speech, capable of being employed for any purpose.

Nevertheless two qualifications must be made. First, the Scots poets of that century, James I, Henryson, and Dunbar, for instance, all regarded themselves as English-speakers; their master was Chaucer, of whom Dunbar wrote:

O reuerend Chaucer, rose of rethoris all,
As in oure tong a flour imperiall.
That raise in Britain evir, who redis rycht,
Thou bearis of makaris the triumph riall ...

It was Dunbar's slightly younger contemporary, Gavin Douglas, the translator of *The Aeneid*, who seems to have been the first to call the language he wrote in 'Scottis'.

Second, below the high literary level, or rather the level of the self-conscious literary artist such as Dunbar or Douglas, there remained little distinction between the tongues employed either side of the political Border. There are only minor linguistic differences between the ballads of Southern Scotland and Northern England, and when he compiled his *Minstrelsy of the Scottish Border*, Scott found nothing incongruous in including *A Lyke-Wake Dirge*, which he described as 'a sort of charm sung by the lower ranks of Roman

Catholics in some parts of the north of England', and *Rose the Red and White Lilly*, which, he suggested, 'may have originally related to the history of the celebrated Robin Hood, as mention is made of Barnisdale, his favourite abode'.

Outwith the areas where the Celtic languages were spoken, there was in the medieval period a common culture binding England and Scotland together. Legends of Arthur (himself of Celtic origin) and Robin Hood are to be found in both countries; and there are English and Scots versions of numerous ballads. Morever, both England and Scotland existed within the one culture of Christendom and were subject to the same influences from Italy and France. Medieval scholars like Michael Scott and Duns Scotus were Europeans in a sense that few have been since the sixteenth century, the former teaching at Palermo, Naples, Toledo and Oxford, the latter at Oxford, Paris and Cologne. The humanists of the Renaissance were no different. John Mair (or Major), for instance, born in North Berwick, was educated at Cambridge and Paris, where he also taught before returning to Scotland to be a professor at successively Glasgow and St Andrews; eight years after Flodden, in his *Historia Majoris Britanniae*, he argued for the union of the crowns of England and Scotland, which, he said, would be to the benefit of both kingdoms, adding that anyone who opposed this could be 'no friend to either nation'.

The Reformation of the sixteenth century not only fractured the unity of Western Christendom; it broke the political alliance between Scotland and France, and brought a new friendly relationship with England into being. Though it is an exaggeration to pretend that Scotland had been engaged in constant wars to maintain her independence from England since the end of the thirteenth century, for warfare was sporadic and as often initiated by the Scots as by the English, nevertheless the Reformation represented a significant shift in our political orientation. For the crucial fact was that protestantism was established in Scotland with the help of English arms and money, and that the reformers looked to England as an ally, and on France as the enemy.

The leading reformer, John Knox, has been described by Gordon Donaldson as 'perhaps the chief agent in all time in the anglicisation of Scotland, in both its politics and its culture'. He had been prominent in the English Reformation of Edward VI's reign, and was indeed offered an English bishopric, which he declined only on account of his 'forewight of trouble to come', the trouble being the probable succession of the Catholic Mary Tudor, against whom (and the Regent of Scotland, Mary of Guise), he directed his *First Blast of the Trumpet against the Monstrous Regiment of Women* ('regiment' of course here meaning 'rule'). He tried to return to England on Mary's death in 1558, only to find himself unwelcome because the new queen, Elizabeth, had been offended by the trumpet blast, Knox not having had the 'forewight' to see that there might be a Protestant queen. Nevertheless it was still to England that he looked for support; his first wife was English and he sent his children to be educated there.

Even more significantly, the Reformation came to Scotland in the English, rather than Scots, version of the common tongue. Though Knox and his fellow-ministers might use a fine racy Scots in their sermons, the Bible, psalter, and service-books which they used were all in the English vernacular. It is impossible to exaggerate the importance of this, for the Bible, eventually in the version authorised by James VI & I in 1611, eight years after the Union of the Crowns, was to be the staple literary diet of the Scottish people for the next three hundred years at least. In the 1930s the poet and critic Edwin Muir was to make the famous assertion that Scots thought in one language and felt in another. This ingenious claim was mistaken, if only because in their most elevated and passionate moments, the language to which a people versed in the Scriptures most naturally had recourse was the language of the King James Bible.

Though we cannot know just how people spoke in the seventeenth century, the language Scott gives his characters in *Old Mortality* is convincing, and in that novel the zealot Mause Headrigg uses a vigorous Scots in her ordinary discourse, but employs Biblical English in her higher and most impassioned flights; and the echo of that language sounds throughout Scottish literature, being especially audible in the tone of such writers as Carlyle, Stevenson, and Buchan. But the same note is heard in many English writers – from Bunyan to Hardy and even D H Lawrence. Cromwell's language was pitched in the same register as that of Covenanting leaders like Alexander Henderson and Johnston of Warriston.

The two countries yoked together in the Union of 1707 had already therefore much in common with each other. The Union secured the Revolution Settlement of 1688-9, and so ended the possibility that an absolute monarchy in the French style could be established in these islands. The protestant religion was safeguarded in both its English and Scottish forms, and parliamentary government, however inadequately representative it might be, and whatever powers the monarchy still retained, was henceforth to be unchallenged. The ruling class, essentially the landed gentry and nobility, recognised a common interest, and Scots were admitted to full equality in the development and expansion of the British Empire. At the end of the eighteenth century when Indian patronage was in the hands of Henry Dundas, first Viscount Melville, Scots benefited disproportionately from this. Although the Treaty of Union was initially unpopular, it was not long before its benefits were felt, and there would have been few to dispute Bailie Nicol Jarvie's estimate of its enriching consequences.

The eighteenth century was then an age of assimilation, and though nationalist Scots now may deplore the willingness of such as David Hume to clear their writings of 'Scotticisms', and though the brief administration of Lord Bute made Scots temporarily unpopular in London, or at least with the Opposition press, one cannot but be struck by the manner in which a common culture was realised.

Two examples are instructive. Dr John Arbuthnott (1667-1735) belonged to the generation already middle-aged at the time of the Union, in support of which he had indeed written a satirical essay, entitled *A Sermon Preached to the People at the Mercat Cross, Edinburgh*. Born in Kincardineshire and educated at the universities of Aberdeen, Oxford, and St Andrews, he had already settled in London where he became physician to Queen Anne. He was a Fellow of the Royal Society, and a close friend of Swift, Pope, and Gay. He was perfectly at ease in London literary society; besides poetry and satirical essays, he published works on medicine and other sciences. The question whether Arbuthnott should be called a Scot living in England, an anglicised Scot, or British, is almost irrelevant. It is probable that he would have thought it meaningless. He fitted comfortably into London life because he shared a common culture with men like Swift and Pope. In the same way, a hundred years earlier, Ben Jonson, of Annandale peasant stock, had dominated the London theatre after Shakespeare's retirement.

The case of James Thomson is even more to the point. Born in 1700 at Ednam in Roxburghshire, where his father was the parish minister, he studied divinity at the university of Edinburgh. In 1725 he moved to London as tutor to the son of the Earl of Haddington, and the next year published the first part of his long poem, *The Seasons*, perhaps the most influential of all the long poems of the century. Its success was immediate, and the young Scot was soon friendly with Pope and Arbuthnott. In his *Companion to Scottish Literature* Trevor Royle calls *The Seasons* 'the pinnacle of the Augustan tradition'. The judgment is sound. Samuel Johnson, the greatest of Augustan critics, declared that 'Thomson thinks always as a man of genius'. Thomson could not conceivably have pleased his age so much had he written as one emerging from a different culture. His success is evidence of the community that existed between Scottish and English taste. It is wholly appropriate that he should also have been the author of *Rule, Britannia*.

It might seem that the enthusiastic reception given to Macpherson's *Ossian* and, later, to Scott's narrative poems and the Waverley novels, flies in the face of the assertion that Thomson's success was the result of a community of culture. Certainly, one attraction of *Ossian* and Scott for English readers lay in their exoticism. But both satisfied and developed a taste that was already there. The origins of Romanticism can be traced a long way back, and the Celts were in vogue before Macpherson gave his conference to the world. Indeed there is a curious parallel to his creation of Ossian. Around 1600 Sir John Wynn, whom Queen Elizabeth had appointed sheriff of Carnarvon, wrote a *History of the Gwidyr Family* to establish his descent from the princess of North Wales. Lacking evidence, which might have been provided if the songs of the Welsh bards had existed or been preserved, he boldly explained its absence by declaring that the bards had all been massacred by Edward I's soldiers. This mythical massacre provided the theme for Thomas Gray's Pindaric Ode, *The Bard*. Gray, usually thought of as a 'typical' Augustan, on the strength of his *Elegy in a Country Churchyard*, was so enamoured of the idea of the Ancient Britons and the Druids that he even took lessons in Welsh. Druids indeed had a deep appeal for the eighteenth-century English. William Collins wrote an Ode on the death of James Thomson which begins: 'In yonder grave a DRUID lies...'. Another ode by Collins, addressed to John Home, author of the tragedy *Douglas, On the Popular Superstitions of the Highlands of Scotland*, has the lines:

> At ev'ry pause, before thy mind possesst,
> Old RUNIC bards shall seem to rise around,
> With uncouth lyres, in many coloured vest,
> Their matted hair with boughs fantastic crown'd ...

Collins, son of a Chichester hatter, and educated at Winchester and Oxford, was undoubtedly English, yet responded enthusiastically to the idea of a Celtic heredity. The ground was well prepared for *Ossian*.

It is well-known of course that Dr Johnson denounced *Ossian* as a fraudulent production (as indeed in large measure it was). But his scepticism was shared by many Scots, among them David Hume, who, writing to congratulate Edward Gibbon on the first volume of his *Decline and Fall of the Roman Empire*, remarked: 'I see you entertain a great doubt with regard to the authenticity of the poems of Ossian. You are certainly right in so doing. It is indeed strange that any men of sense could have imagined it possible, that above twenty thousand verses, along with numberless historical facts, could have been preserved by oral tradition, during fifty generations, by the rudest, perhaps, of all the European nations, the most necessitous, the most turbulent, and the most unsettled'. We know more about the persistence of oral tradition now than either Hume or Gibbon did, and have stronger evidence of its capacity for retention, but that does not alter the fact that on this subject the Englishman and the Lowland Scot found themselves in easy agreement.

Hume and Gibbon had more in common than the scepticism they displayed towards Ossian. Both were influenced and stimulated by the idea of 'philosophic history' developed by Montesquieu, who sought to explain political and religious forms by geographical and social causes. Of Montesquieu's ideas, Hugh Trevor-Roper has written: 'Their most immediate effect was not in England, where intellectual life was stagnant after the Whig triumph of 1715; it was in Scotland, where the mental discipline of a Calvinist society suddenly found itself – in consequence of the Union of 1707 – in fertile contact with a maturer world'. It may be disputed with some reason whether this was indeed in consequence of the Union, though it may also be argued that Montesquieu's suggestion that cultural association was as important as political structures had a special force in Scotland in the circumstances prevailing after the Union. But if Hume and Robertson showed the way, Gibbon, writing from the same principles, surpassed them, for he is the only historian of the Enlightenment who is still read as a historian. Yet the Scottish historians, as well as Montesquieu, Voltaire, and the French Encyclopaedists, all contributed to his development: an example of the cross-fertilisation characteristic of the relations between France, England, and Scotland.

Of course the Union had set up tensions. It could not be otherwise. Even though they may be considered for the most part to have been fruitful, few Scots will not, at some moments, respond to Cockburn's lament that the eighteenth century

> was the last purely Scotch age. Most of what had gone before had been turbulent and political. All that has come after has been English. The eighteenth century was the final Scotch century. We whose youth tasted

the close of that century and who lived far into the Southern influence, feel proud of a purely Edinburgh society which raised the reputation of our discrowned capital and graced the deathbed of our national manners.

Yet nostalgia of this sort, however attractive, is always vitiated by sentimentality. It is on a par with Rosebery's assertion that 'the Scots are still Jacobites at heart'. Cockburn himself after all played a conspicuous part in the assimilation of Scotland and England. He was a lifelong friend and associate of Francis Jeffrey, the dominant editor of the *Edinburgh Review*, which laid down canons of taste eagerly welcomed on either side of the Border. Moreover, Cockburn was Solicitor-General and Jeffrey Lord Advocate in the Whig Government which passed the Reform Act of 1832, that established a uniform franchise throughout the UK. Five years earlier Cockburn had applauded the instruction given by the Tory Prime Minister Canning to his Home Secretary to oversee the administration of Scotland, and expressed himself delighted at the end of 'the horrid system of being ruled by a nasty jobbing Scot'. The Whigs reformed the Scottish burghs and the universities, again eliding differences between Scottish and English systems. Michael Fry, in a valuable essay, *The Whig Interpretation of Scottish History* (1992) observes that while the Whigs 'lauded the basically English nature' (of the post-Union constitution), 'they saw its local Scottish elements as deformities, excrescences of Scotland's black feudal past'. Modernisation for Cockburn and Jeffrey meant assimilation.

Events on the Continent had done much to strengthen the idea of Britain. The great event of the age had been the French Revolution. Cockburn again remarked that 'everything rung, or was connected with the Revolution in France; which, for twenty years was, or was made, the all in all. Everything, not this or that thing, but literally everything was soaked in this one event'; which, one might add, was welcomed and abhorred in like manner in both England and Scotland. Moreover, it was an Irishman, Burke, who in his *Reflections on the Revolution in France*, argued for the superiority of the organic British political tradition over the French theories which were experimental and rational. Sir Walter Scott found nothing incongruous in admitting Nelson and Wellington to a Pantheon of heroes in which Wallace and Bruce were already installed.

The fullest expression of triumphant and intelligent Unionism was to be given by Macaulay in his *History of England*. Macaulay himself could not be called properly either Scots or English. His father, Zachary, was a Highlander by birth, who had gone to Jamaica at an early age and devoted the rest of his life to the abolition of the slave trade. He was an Evangelical, a member of the Clapham Sect, and married to the Quaker daughter of a Bristol bookseller. He was also, like many Evangelicals, a Tory. The young Macaulay reacted against his religious and political background, becoming after a flirtation with Radicalism at Cambridge, an Establishment Whig of the Holland House variety, which drew its inspiration partly from Burke, but chiefly from Charles Fox. Macaulay made his name first as an essayist, writing for the *Edinburgh Review*, then by his speeches in favour of parliamentary reform. He spent five years, 1834-8, in India as a member of the Supreme Council, where he was responsible for decreeing that Indians should be educated in the English language and in the British legal and political tradition. Subsequently he was Member of Parliament for Edinburgh 1839-47 and 1852-6. He held Cabinet Office and was also Rector of Glasgow University.

In his *History*, he wrote of the Union: 'Scotland had, with heroic energy, vindicated her independence, had, from the time of Robert Bruce, been a separate kingdom, and was now joined to the southern part of the island in a manner which rather gratified than wounded her national pride'. He admitted that 'the sacrifice could not but be painfully felt' by many, and that 'there were doubtless many punctilious patriots who would have strenuously opposed a union even if they could have seen that the effect of a union would be to make Glasgow a greater city than Amsterdam, and to cover the dreary Lothians with harvests and woods, neat farmhouses and stately mansions'. Nevertheless the Union had been beneficial because the English had treated Scottish national institutions with respect, and had held Scotland's religious and educational systems in the same high regard as the Scots themselves. Consequently, 'in Scotland all the great actions of the two races are thrown into the common stock, and are considered as making up the glory which belongs to the whole country'. Macaulay himself was after all the personification of the benefits of union; his Indian legislation was intended to develop the same harmony of sentiment and culture which he recognized as having been achieved within the UK.

No one influenced Macaulay the historian more than Scott, who, in his novels, was himself the heir of the philosophic historians of the Enlightenment. 'Sir Walter Scott', Macaulay wrote, 'has used these fragments of truth, which historians have scornfully thrown behind them, in a manner which may well excite their envy. He has constructed out of their gleanings works which, even considered as histories, are scarcely less valuable than theirs. But a truly great historian would reclaim those materials which the novelist has appropriated'. He set himself to do so; his *History of England* and his *Essays* testify to the cross-fertilisation, not only between history and the novel, but, more pertinently to my argument, between Scotland and England which has been a feature of our relationship.

Macaulay's great contemporary, Carlyle, offers an even better illustration of this. Carlyle was thoroughly Scots in family, upbringing, and education, though the chief intellectual influence on him was to be the German Romantics, and though he reacted against what he saw as the complacency of the Enlightenment – Scotch as well as French. But, when he settled in London, he made himself for at least a dozen years, the greatest moral force in England. His *Past and Present* (1843) was the great indictment of the Industrial System, and the economic theories which derived from Adam Smith. He identified 'a deep-seated struggle in the whole fabric of society; a boundless grinding collision between the old and the new'. Though no novelist himself, he inspired numerous novels dealing with 'the Condition of England', in the 1840s. (If there were fewer in Scotland, it was perhaps because the year of the publication of *Past and Present* was also the year of the Disruption of the Church, an event which was to dominate debate in Scotland for a long time.) Carlyle's influence in England however was such that in 1855 George Eliot was to write that 'there is hardly a superior or active mind of this generation that has not been modified by Carlyle's writings; there has hardly been an English book written for the last ten or twelve years which would not have been different if Carlyle had not lived'.

There could scarcely be more cogent testimony, from a more convincing source, to the great, if often wilfully obscured, truth, that cultural influence has been exerted in both directions across the border between England and Scotland. The theoretical and practical sciences, being by their nature international, may fairly be excluded from this argument, though any attempt to deny the influence of Scottish scientists and engineers on English life and culture would be absurd. Yet, even making this huge exception, the influence of Scotland on England has been at least as great as the influence of England on Scotland. It is hard to think of three Englishmen who have so affected the way Scotsmen think and feel as Adam Smith, Walter Scott, and Thomas Carlyle have influenced and formed our southern neighbour. What is called English culture very often has its roots in Scotland; a novelist as apparently wholly English as Evelyn Waugh was descended not only from Berwickshire Waughs, but also from Cockburn himself. The anarchic style of his comedy, his ability to switch abruptly from a high rhetorical style to demotic farce, recalls Byron ('born half a Scot and bred a whole one'), and reveals that delight in opposites which has been identified as a Scottish characteristic. Like MacDiarmid, Waugh would have 'nae hauf-way hoose, but aye be whaur extremes meet'. His equally English friend and fellow-novelist, Graham Greene, was proud of his kinship with Stevenson.

One could multiply examples. I have said nothing for instance of the influence exerted by Scottish journalists through their dominance of Fleet Street on English life and thought. I have no space to say anything of the part played by Scots in English university education, though that could be the subject of a book as important as George Davie's *The Democratic Intellect*, which describes how Scottish universities were reformed under English influences. I could devote time to showing how that most characteristically British/English institution, the BBC, was formed in accordance with the inherited Calvinism of its first and greatest Director-General, John Reith. I might in like manner dilate on the apparent irony that the greatest record of the English language, the *Oxford English Dictionary* – that linguistic cathedral which can never be completed – is still compiled according to the principles laid down, and the method developed, by its first editor Sir James Murray, the son of a tailor in the little Roxburghshire village of Denholm, and how Murray had already practised the same method in his first book, *The Dialect of the Southern Counties of Scotland*.

Yet this might be superfluous, for, as I have tried to show, the irony is more apparent than real, since the connection between England and Scotland has been so prolonged, so deep, and so fruitful. To say this is not to deny that a distinct Scottish culture exists, as a distinct English one does. It is not to suggest that both are smothered by a British culture. Even to say, as those who opposed the Scotland Act in 1978-9 said, that 'Scotland is British' is not to deny that it is also Scottish. The truth is that we live within a network of cultures, extending from the local level, yet each playing off all others and contributing to them. Our culture is Scottish, but it is also British, just as it is also European; but the relationship between the different parts of the British Isles have been so close for so long that it is often hard to be certain which influence is dominant at any moment or in any place. What I have tried to show is the community that exists between the varieties of culture identifiable within these islands. I might add that there has been so much migration within Great Britain and Ireland over the last centuries that even national identity is frequently a matter of choice: Compton Mackenzie, for instance, educated at St Paul's and Magdalen College, Oxford, began as a very English London and Home Counties novelist, then decided in middle age that he was a Scotsman, became one of the founders of the Scottish National Party, and ended as the Grand Old Man of Scottish letters. (Nevertheless, his best writing is set in the south.)

John Buchan, son of a Free Kirk minister in the Gorbals, but of Border stock, moved in the other direction, while remaining intensely Scottish. Yet when he bought an Oxford manor-house after the First World War, he wrote of it in his autobiography:

> Now I 'took sasine'" (a phrase from Scots law) of English soil, and learned to know intimately what I had hitherto only admired. Especially I came to respect the English countrymen who had been the backbone of our army in the War, and has always been the backbone of the nation. I delighted in his slow idiomatic speech, his firm hold on the past, his fortitude and kindliness. Indeed, I think these early years at Elsfield were the happiest of my life, for I acquired a new loyalty and a new heritage, having added the southern Midlands to the Scottish Borders. I loved
>
> > 'with equal mind
> > The southern sun, the northern wind,
> > The lilied lowland watermead,
> > And the grey hills that cradle Tweed;'
>
> and felt amazingly rich in consequence.

We all, to some extent, and in different ways, can partake of that richness if we acknowledge what we owe to each other either side of the border. It may be that Scotland and England will drift apart politically; I rather think we shall. If we do so, there will be gains, which others have insisted on so vehemently that I feel no need to recite them here. But there will also be losses, incalculable but profound, if political separation encourages us to deny the community of culture that binds us to 'our sister and ally'. Yet these bonds of shared experience, familial relationships, and cultural community are so strong and so intricately woven that it seems improbable that political action can either sever or disentangle them. A greater and more immediate danger is that political enthusiasm will seek to deny their existence, and to construct a false history to replace them. Such history, being founded on intellectual dishonesty, can only be harmful. If Scotland is to assume political independence, we can only avoid damage to ourselves by first acknowledging the reality of the common inheritance that goes by the name of Britain. We shall be less Scottish if we pretend that we are not also British.

Notes

David King, **Economic Independence and Political Independence**

1. Ash and Bell (1991) have suggested that in 1989, for example, a 1% rise in interest rates would reduce per capita disposable income net of interest payments by £163 in the south east and £77 in Scotland.
2. *Regional Trends 28* 1993 edition (London: HMSO) 132, gives GDP per head figures for Scotland and the UK in sterling. The Scottish figures have been adjusted upwards by 0.05% to reach estimates of GNP, and then adjusted to dollars in proportion to the UK figure shown on Table 2.
3. Some economists might use the notion of Ricardian equivalence to ask if there is a problem here with debt finance. Might not Scottish residents, knowing that taxes would one day rise to enable the debt to be repaid, at once cut spending and raise saving, and thereby bequeath extra savings to their children who would have to pay the extra taxes? Against this only two points need be made: first, that there is very limited evidence to support the view that people would behave like this, and second, that if they did, it would mean that attempts to stimulate the Scottish economy by deficit finance would be rendered useless because government spending increases (or tax cuts) would be offset by higher saving.
4. It is interesting to note that the UK's public sector debt was only 35.4% of GDP in 1991 when the Maastricht Treaty was signed; but it is forecast to rise to 52.5% by 1994 (figures from OECD *Economic Outlook* 53, June 1993, 141).

John Thomson, **The Foreign Dimension: Choices for Scots**

1. This is a conservative estimate. Some authorities quote 5,000 and others go as high as 7,000.
2. Burma might be considered an exception to this view. She has symbolized her self-chosen state of isolation (she resigned from the Non-Aligned Movement for example) by changing her name to Myanmar. But her current situation does not suggest that the result is a happy one, either for the Burmese nation or for the inhabitants of Myanmar. And there are signs that the government is beginning to recognize this and to wish to rejoin the world.
3. For the purposes of this essay, as elsewhere in the book, the term 'EU' is used throughout, despite the messy situation in which it is sometimes correct and sometimes incorrect to refer to the European Union. For example, unlike the European Community, the European Union does not enjoy international legal personality and yet the Community is within the Union. To be even more pedantic, the European Community which was previously known as the European Economic Community is one of three institutions within the European Communities

(plural), the other two organisations dealing with Coal and Steel on the one hand and Atomic Energy on the other. In addition to the European Communities (plural), the European Union covers intergovernmental cooperation in a common foreign and security policy and similar cooperation in justice and home affairs. The reader is asked to bear with such minor inexactitudes as the constant use of 'EU' may occasion.

4. The exchange rate used for the conversion of Danish kroner to pounds sterling is that prevailing on 1 October 1993, namely 1 Dkr = £0.1005.

5. The diplomatic and defence budgets include the 'subscriptions' to NATO and to the UN which were mentioned above.

6. The vexed question of the possible division of North Sea oil and gas revenues is a special subject outside the scope of this essay.

7. The term is used here in its normal broad sense, meaning essentially the 25 OECD countries. While these countries (including Japan) remain the core, it is evident that in the present conditions of flux other countries may to a greater or lesser extent attach themselves to the West.

8. The G7 (Group of Seven) was established in 1975 with the USA, Canada, Japan, the UK, France, Germany and Italy as members. The President of the EU is in attendance. It began well, but has languished.

Colin R Munro, The Union of 1707 and the British Constitution

1. First, because they were *obiter*. Second, because the Lord Advocate conceded the point, so no opposing submission was argued: by contrast, in the later case of *Gibson v Lord Advocate* 1975 SC 136, the Lord Advocate denied in his argument that the Court of Session had jurisdiction to interfere with an Act of Parliament on the ground of its inconsistency with the legislation. More generally, it may be argued that Lord Cooper relies on a false premise, as it is not clear that the Scottish Parliament (the authority of which had grown rapidly since 1688) lacked attributes which the English Parliament had in 1707.

Bibliography

Abbott, W. C., (1937-1947). *The writings and speeches of Oliver Cromwell*. 4 vols. Cambridge, Mass: Harvard University Press.

Anderson, B., (1991). *Imagined communities*. Cambridge: Verso.

Anderson, R. D., (1989). *Education and opportunity in Victorian Scotland*. Edinburgh: Edinburgh University Press.

Ash, C., and Bell, D. N. F., (1991). *The regional impact of changes in interest rates*. Discussion paper in economics 91/5. Stirling: University of Stirling.

Bell Lawrie White/Pieda (1992). *The act of dis-union of 1992*. Edinburgh.

Brown, K. M., (1990). Courtiers and cavaliers: service, anglicization and loyalty among the royalist nobility. In *The Scottish national covenant in its British context*, ed J Morrill. Edinburgh: John Donald.

Cabinet Office (1987). *The judge over your shoulder*. London: HMSO.

Calvert, H., (1968). *Constitutional law in Northern Ireland*. London: Stevens

Calvert, H., (1970). Northern Ireland: what went wrong? In *Welsh studies in public law*, ed J A Andrews. Cardiff: University of Wales Press

Campbell, R. H., (1980). *The rise and fall of Scottish industry 1707-1939*. Edinburgh: John Donald.

Charles II (1651). *The forme and coronation of Charles the second, king of Scotland, England, France and Ireland*. Edinburgh.

Colley, L., (1992). *Britons: forging the nation 1707-1837*. New Haven: Yale University Press.

Cowan, E. J., (1980). The union of the crowns and the crisis of the constitution. In *The satellite state in the seventeenth century*, edd S Dyrvik *et al.* Oslo.

Daiches, D., (1977). *Scotland and the union*. London: John Murray.

Dalyell, T., (1977). *Devolution: the end of Britain*. London: Jonathan Cape.

Davie, G. E., (1961). *The democratic intellect*. Edinburgh: Edinburgh University Press.

Davies, R. R., (1988). *The British isles 1100-1500*. Edinburgh: John Donald.

Defoe, D., (1709). *The history of the Union of Great Britain*. Edinburgh.

Dicey, A. V., (1967). *An introduction to the study of the law of the constitution*. 10th edition. London: Macmillan.

Donaldson, G., (1985). Foundations of the Anglo-Scottish union. In *Scottish Church History*. Edinburgh: Scottish Academic Press.

Ferguson, W., (1977). *Scotland's relations with England*. Edinburgh: John Donald.

Flynn, J., (1986). A simulation model of the effects of exchange rate changes on inflation and the trade balance. *Central Bank of Ireland Quarterly Bulletin 2*.

Frame, R., (1990). *The political development of the British isles*. Oxford: Oxford University Press.

Franck, T. M., (1968). *Why federations fail*. New York: New York University Press.

Fraser, W. I. R., (1948). *Outline of constitutional law*. 2nd ed. Edinburgh: W Green & Son.

Galloway, B. R., (1986). *The union of England and Scotland 1603-1608*. Edinburgh: John Donald.

Henderson, D., (1992). International economic integration. *International Affairs*, **68**(4), 633-653.

Hobsbawm, E. J., (1990). *Nations and nationalism since 1780*. Cambridge: Verso.

Hume Brown, P., (1914). *The legislative union of England and Scotland*. London: Oxford University Press.

Huntington, S. P., (1993). The clash of civilizations? *Foreign Affairs*, **72**(3), 22-49.

Institute of Public Policy Research (1993). *The constitution of the United Kingdom.* London.

Jennings, W. I., (1953). *Some characteristics of the Indian constitution*. London: Oxford University Press.

Jennings, W. I., (1959). *The law and the constitution*. 5th edition. London: University of London Press.

Jerviswood Correspondence (1842). *The correspondence of George Baillie of Jerviswood 1702-1708*. Edinburgh: Bannatyne Club.

JTC (1961). Summoning the estates: law and fact. *Scots Law Times (News)*, 98.

Kilbrandon Report (1973). *Report of the Royal Commission on the Constitution 1969-1973*. Cmnd 5460. London: HMSO.

King, D. N., (1973). *Economic aspects of regionalism and separatism.* Commission on the Constitution Research Papers 10. London: HMSO.

King, D. N., (1980). *Models of devolution*. Discussion papers in economics, Finance and Investment 83. Stirling: University of Stirling.

King, D. N., (1981) *Stabilization and subcentral government*. Discussion papers in economics, Finance and Investment 89. Stirling: University of Stirling.

King, D. N., (1984). *Fiscal tiers: the economics of multi-level government*. London: Allen & Unwin.

Lane, R. C., (1991). Scotland in Europe: an independent Scotland and the European Community. In *Edinburgh essays in public law*, edd W Finnie, C M G Himsworth and N C Walker. Edinburgh: Edinburgh University Press.

Laski, H. J., (1939). The obsolescence of federalism. *The New Republic*, **98**, 367.

Leddin, A. J., and Walsh, B. M., (1990). *The macroeconomy of Ireland*. Dublin: Gill & Macmillan.

Levack, B. P., (1987). *The formation of the British state*. Oxford: Clarendon Press.

Lyall, F., (1980). *Of presbyters and kings*. Aberdeen: Aberdeen University Press.

MacCormick, D. N., (1978). Does the United Kingdom have a constitution? *Northern Ireland Legal Quarterly*, **29**, 1.

MacCormick, D. N., (1994). What place for nationalism in the modern world? In *In search of new constitutions*, Hume Papers on Public Policy **2**(1). Edinburgh: Edinburgh University Press for The David Hume Institute.

McCrie, T., (1842). *The life of Mr Robert Blair*. Edinburgh.

McCrone, D., (1992). *Understanding Scotland: the sociology of a stateless nation*. London: Routledge.

MacQueen, H. L., (1993). *Common law and feudal society in medieval Scotland*. Edinburgh: Edinburgh University Press.

Marquand, D., (1989). Regional devolution. In *The changing constitution*, edd J Jowell and D Oliver, 2nd edition. Oxford: Clarendon Press.

Marr, A., (1992). *The battle for Scotland*. London: Penguin Books.

Marshall, G., (1957). *Parliamentary sovereignty and the commonwealth*. Oxford: Oxford University Press.

Middleton, K. W. B., (1954). New thoughts on the union. *Juridical Review* **66**, 37.

Minogue, K. R., (1967). *Nationalism*. London: Batsford.

Mitchell, J. D. B., (1956). Book review. *Public Law*, **1**, 294.

Mitchell, J. D. B., (1968). *Constitutional law*. 2nd ed. Edinburgh: W Green & Son.

Morrill, J., (1993). The Britishness of the English revolution. In *Three nations – a common history?*, ed R Asch. Bochum.

Morrill, J., (1994). A British patriarchy? Ecclesiastical imperialism under the early Stuarts. In *Religion, culture and society in early modern Britain*, edd A Fletcher and P Roberts. Cambridge: Cambridge University Press.

Munro, C. R., (1983). What is a constitution? *Public Law*, **28**, 563.

Munro, C. R., (1987). *Studies in constitutional law*. London: Butterworths.

Munro, C. R., (1994). The British constitution in the 1990s. *Coexistence*, **31**, 1.

Musgrave, R. A., (1959). *The theory of public finance*. New York: McGraw-Hill.

Olson, M., (1982). *The rise and decline of nations*. New Haven, USA: Yale University Press.

Peacock, A., and Bannock, G., (1991). *Corporate takeovers and the public interest*. Aberdeen: Aberdeen University Press for The David Hume Institute.

Pocock, J. G. A., (1975). British history: a plea for a new subject. *Journal of Modern History*, **4**, 619.

Pocock, J. G. A., (1982). The limits and divisions of British history. *American Historical Review*, **87**(2), 317.

Rait, R. S., (1924). *The parliaments of Scotland*. Glasgow: Maclehose Jackson & Co.

Renton Report (1975). *Report on the preparation of legislation*. Cmnd 6053. London: HMSO.

Reynolds, A., (1992). Talking with Albert Reynolds. In M. Parkin and D. N. King, *Economics*. Wokingham: Addison-Wesley.

Riker, W. H., (1964). *Federalism*. Boston.

Riley, P. W. J., (1974). The structure of Scottish politics and the union of 1707. In *The union of 1707* ed T I Rae. Glasgow: Blackie & Son.

Riley, P. W. J., (1978). *The union of England and Scotland*. Manchester: Manchester University Press.

Rodger, A. F., (1992). The codification of commercial law in Victorian Britain. *Law Quarterly Review*, **108**, 570.

Sawer, G., (1976). *Modern federalism*. 2nd edition. Carlton, Australia: Pitman.

Scott, P. H. (1991). *Towards independence: essays on Scotland*. Edinburgh: Polygon.

Scott, P. H., (1992a). *Scotland in Europe: dialogue with a sceptical friend*. Edinburgh.

Scott, P. H., (1992b). *Andrew Fletcher and the treaty of union*. Edinburgh: John Donald.

Scottish Constitutional Convention (1990). *Key elements for proposals for a Scottish parliament*. Edinburgh.

Scottish Office (1937). *Report of the committee on Scottish administration*. Cmnd 5563. London: HMSO.

Scottish Office (1993). *Scotland and the union: a partnership for good*. Cm 2225. London: HMSO.

Sellar, W. D. H., (1988). The common law of Scotland and the common law of England. In Davies 1988.

Seton-Watson, H., (1977). *Nations and states: an enquiry into the origins of nations and the politics of nationalism*. London: Methuen

Smith, T. B., (1953). Two Scots cases. *Law Quarterly Review*, **69**, 512.

Smith, T. B., (1957). The union of 1707 as fundamental law. *Public Law* **2**, 99.

Smith, T. B., (1961). *British justice: the Scottish contribution*. London: Sweet & Maxwell.

Smith, T. B., (1962). *A short commentary on the law of Scotland*. Edinburgh: W Green & Son.

Smith, T. B., (1987). Fundamental law. *The laws of Scotland: Stair memorial encyclopedia*, 5, paras 338-360. Edinburgh: Butterworths.

Smout, T. C., (1963). *Scottish trade on the eve of union 1660-1707* (Edinburgh, 1963)

Smout, T. C., (1969). The road to union. In G.S. Holmes (ed), *Britain after the glorious revolution* ed G. S. Holmes. London.

Smout, T. C., (1977). The Scottish identity. In *The future of Scotland*, ed R Underwood. London: Croom Helm for The Nevis Institute.

Smout, T. C., (1987). *A century of the Scottish people 1830-1950*. London: Fontana.

Speck, W. A., (1994). *The birth of Britain: a new nation 1700-1710*. Oxford: Blackwells.

Stevenson, D., (1990). Cromwell, Scotland and Ireland. In *Oliver Cromwell and the English revolution*, ed J Morrill. London.

Storrar, W., (1990). *Scottish identity: a Christian vision*. Edinburgh: Handsell Press.

Trevelyan, G. M., (1932). *Ramillies and the union with Scotland*. London: Longmans Green & Co.

Upton, M., (1989). Marriage vows of the elephant. *Law Quarterly Review*, 105, 79.

Various authors (1991). *The constitution of the United Kingdom*. Institute for Public Policy Research, London.

Walker, N. C., and Himsworth, C. M. G., (1991). The poll tax and fundamental law. *Juridical Review*, 36, 45.

Walsh, B. M., (1987). Why is unemployment so high? In *Perspectives on Economic Policy* 1. Dublin: Centre for Economic Research, University College.

Wendt, H., (1993). *Global embrace: corporate challenges in a transnational world*. New York: Harper Business.

Wheare, K. C., (1963). *Federal government*. 4th edition. London: Oxford University Press.

Williamson, A. H., (1979). *Scottish national consciousness in the age of James VI*. Edinburgh: John Donald.

World Bank (1993). *World development report 1993*. Oxford: Oxford University Press.